The REST *of the* GOSPEL

The REST of the GOSPEL

DAN STONE
DAVID GREGORY

HARVEST HOUSE PUBLISHERS
EUGENE, OREGON

Cover by Left Coast Design, Portland, Oregon

David Gregory is represented by MacGregor Literary, Inc. of Hillsboro, Oregon.

THE REST OF THE GOSPEL
Copyright © 2000 by David Gregory Smith
Published by Harvest House Publishers
Eugene, Oregon 97408
www.harvesthousepublishers.com

Library of Congress Cataloging-in-Publication Data
    Gregory, David, 1959-
    The rest of the gospel / David Gregory and Dan Stone.
        pages cm
    ISBN 978-0-7369-5638-3 (pbk.)
    ISBN 978-0-7369-5639-0 (eBook)
    1. Christian life. I. Title.
    BV4501.3.G7435 2014
    248.4—dc23

                                                    2013018545

Printed in the United States of America

19 20 21 22 / VP-JH / 10 9 8 7 6

To Barbara Stone, my wife, whose simple question one day,
"Dan, what would you do if you could do anything you wanted to?
And don't stop to think about your answer,"
led to more than fifteen years of travel together,
sharing the good news of "Christ in you, the hope of glory."
Barbara died January 22, 1993, of cancer.—DS

To my best friend, my strongest support,
an unexpected gift from God who exceeds all my dreams:
Ava, my wife. What a wonder you are.—DG

Contents

Part Five: *Living in Union*

PREFACE

I first met Dan Stone at a retreat near Tyler, Texas. His message of the believer's union with Jesus Christ was not entirely new to me, but through him the Holy Spirit began opening the eyes of my heart anew to this wonderful reality. So has He used Dan in the lives of countless others to usher them into a deeper experience of "Christ in you, the hope of glory."

Years later, I proposed to Dan that I put his teaching into book form. He graciously supported the project, which has resulted in this book. The book is written in the first person, as from Dan. The primary content is Dan's, although he instructed me to note that he disclaims any originality of the material. So noted. My contribution has been to organize, supplement, and clarify—and to be repeatedly blessed by the content myself.

Dan went home to the Lord in October 2005. God has continued to use his teaching in the lives of tens of thousands both in America and abroad through more than ten translations of the book. I am thrilled that Harvest House Publishers has decided to release a new version of the book to an even wider audience.

May the Lord be pleased to use this book to cause "the growth of the body for the building up of itself in love" (Ephesians 4:16). And may you drink deeply of the water of life who is Christ, "know[ing] the love of Christ which surpasses knowledge, that you may be filled up to all the fullness of God" (Ephesians 3:19).

David Gregory
August 2013

INTRODUCTION

I spent 24 years traveling around the country talking to people about the mystery of the gospel: "Christ in you, the hope of glory" (Colossians 1:27). Christ living in us and through us, as us, is the only hope we have of experiencing the glory God intends for our lives. David Gregory and I have written this book to help you enter into Christ's fullness in your life.

There is a flip side to "the hope of glory," however. Yes, Christ in us is our only hope of experiencing God's glory ourselves. But it is also the way that God has chosen to glorify Himself through us. As DeVern Fromke writes in *Ultimate Intention*, God has chosen to eternally manifest His glory by living His life in and through a host of sons and daughters. I want to begin this book by discussing not the glory we receive from God, but the glory He receives through us.

Christian books always run the risk of being man-centered. Most are addressed to a specific human need or to our deep, universal need of intimacy with God. Addressing man's needs, many Christian books, as well as much Christian teaching and thought, essentially begin with man and implicitly portray God as man's need-meeter.

If we don't begin from God's point of view, we end up with man at the center. That's true even in our approach to the Word of God. We often read the beginning of Genesis and focus immediately on the fall of man into sin. The rest of Scripture chronicles God's redemption of man. All of which is true. It can appear, however, and is often preached, that God's ultimate purpose is the rescue of man. The result is a focus on us and our need.

But if we begin before the foundation of the world, before Genesis 1:1, we start from another point of view. We start with this question:

what is God's intent? Answering that question is like Galileo or Coper-
nicus discovering that the earth wasn't at the center of the universe (or
at least our solar system). The sun was. We are not the center of the universe. The Son is.

It's easy to live as if we are the center of the universe. We would never
say it, or even think it consciously, but we can live as if God is here for
us. That has come across in a lot of "Christian" teaching. God is here to
bless you. You ought to be rich. You ought to be prosperous. It's your due
to be successful. It's your due to get ahead. God has to respond to your
faith. God has obligated Himself to bless you if you do the right things.
All of which means what? *You* are the center of the universe.

If we start before the foundation of the world, though, we discover
that God has a plan—a plan conceived before time began. Paul revealed
God's plan most clearly in the first chapter of Ephesians.

> Blessed be the God and Father of our Lord Jesus Christ, who
> has blessed us with every spiritual blessing in the heavenly
> places in Christ...(1:3)

Is it God's intent to bless us? Absolutely. He has already blessed us
with every possible blessing in the heavenly realm.

> ...just as He chose us in Him before the foundation of the
> world...(1:4a)

God had a purpose for us before the foundation of the world. He
chose us for that purpose.

> ...that we would be holy and blameless before Him. In love
> He predestined us to adoption as sons through Jesus Christ
> to Himself...(1:4b-5a)

God's plan involved having a host of sons (and daughters) who
would be holy and blameless in His sight. Through the subjection of
the Son to the cross, God intended to bring many children into glory
(Hebrews 2:10). Why? Paul continued:

> ...according to the kind intention of His will, to the praise of

the glory of His grace, which He freely bestowed on us in the Beloved (1:5b-6).

To make sure we don't miss the point, Paul repeated it six verses later:

...to the end that we who were the first to hope in Christ would be to the praise of His glory (1:12).

And two verses after that:

[The Holy Spirit] is given as a pledge of our inheritance, with a view to the redemption of God's own possession, to the praise of His glory (1:14).

We exist for the praise of His glory. God "works all things after the counsel of His will" (1:11b) to accomplish that purpose. And what exactly is it that glorifies God? What has He set out to accomplish from before the foundation of the world?

In all wisdom and insight He made known to us the mystery of His will, according to His kind intention which He purposed in [Christ] with a view to an administration suitable to the fullness of the times, that is, the summing up of all things in Christ, things in the heavens and things on the earth (1:8-10).

God's plan was to bring into being a host of sons and daughters whom He would indwell, through whom He would live and manifest Himself, and in and through whom Christ would reign supreme. We are the beneficiaries of that plan. God, in His love and grace, has made us a part of His plan. But we are not the center of it; Christ is. We are participants in the plan, participants God loves and cherishes and nourishes, as a husband does his bride (Ephesians 5:25-32).

We are God's inheritance. We tend to focus on what we inherit in Christ, but the greater truth is that we are *His* inheritance:

I pray that the eyes of your heart may be enlightened, so that you will know...what are the riches of the glory of His inheritance in the saints (Ephesians 1:18).

His inheritance is His body—the Body of Christ—accomplishing His purpose. And though the Bible records man's fall, that calamity did not do one thing to delay or alter God's purpose. His intention was always to have a vast family of sons and daughters. The fall didn't change that intention. God incorporates our redemption into that plan, but the plan's goal is still the same. We are here for the praise of His glory.

Romans 11:36 amplifies this marvelous truth:

> For from Him and through Him and to Him are all things.
> To Him be the glory forever.

From: everything comes from God. *Through:* by means of Him. And *to:* the ultimate end is unto Him—not Him unto us, but us unto Him.

In *The Rest of the Gospel* we say that everything we need to know for experiencing God's abundant life is found in the cross of Christ. We look at the cross and see what God did for us there. Praise God that is true. That was Christ's work on our behalf.

Even more than that, though, the cross was God's work on His own behalf. Through the cross God accomplished what He needed to fulfill His own eternal purposes, that all things might be summed up in Christ.

"Christ in you, the hope of glory" is primarily *His* glory. Christ lives in us to manifest His life through us. Christ in us accomplishes His own purposes. Part of His purpose is intimacy with us, but His plan encompasses more than that. He is working toward His own ends, and we are the vessels through which He works. We are the visible manifestation of what God is doing, with Himself as the ultimate goal, "that God may be all in all" (1 Corinthians 15:28).

That's why the Father wants us to be "filled up to all the fullness of God." And that's what *The Rest of the Gospel* is about: being filled to all the fullness of God, to the praise of His glory.

Part One

Union with Christ

1

The Gates

Most people's Christianity is like an old iron bed: firm at both ends and sagging in the middle. On one end you trust Christ as Savior and get your sins forgiven. On the other end, one day you will die and go to heaven. In between, it gets pretty desperate. You have lots of questions that all boil down to one: Where is the abundant life Jesus promised?

Jesus met a man with such a question. The Bible calls him <u>the rich young ruler</u>. One day he came to Jesus and asked, "Teacher, what shall I do to inherit eternal life?"

Jesus said to him, "You know the commandments. Don't murder. Don't commit adultery. Don't steal. Don't bear false witness. Honor your father and mother."

The young man replied, "I've kept all those commandments."

I always say, Jesus wasn't a Baptist preacher. If He had been a Baptist preacher (like me), He'd have said, "There's no way you could have kept them. You know you've broken them. You know you've looked lustfully at a woman."

Jesus didn't say that. He took him at his word: "I've kept all those commandments." But the real question was still on the man's heart. "Where is the life?"

Where is the life? The same question so many Christians ask today. Yes, I received Christ, but isn't there more to life than what I'm experiencing?

Where is true life? Jesus said, "The gate is small and the way is narrow that leads to life" (Matthew 7:14). He said the life He gives is abundant, fulfilling, freeing, wonderful. And though there is a gate that leads to this life, Jesus went on to say, "There are few who find it."

It's there. It's real. But few find it.

I've found that there is a series of gates along the path to life. These gates are the progression from being a completely external person (trying to find life in things and people around us) to being an internal person, finding life in the One who lives within us. These gates are unique to each person. Let me tell you about mine.

Before I came to Christ, my whole life, like everyone's, was based on externals. When we are without Christ, we perceive life in things or people and we live on those externals. I didn't know who I was except in relation to the external things in my life. I was in my early twenties and took my entire identity from the crowd I hung out with: our dress, our conduct, our activities.

One Sunday morning, after a long night on the town, I struggled into church to be with a girl I liked. God lured me through a trap called "female." At that point I was still outside my first gate. I hadn't even begun the journey from external to internal, because I hadn't received Jesus Christ by faith as my Savior.

The young preacher that morning was inside that first gate, though. He had already received Christ, and he was proclaiming the good news that "Christ died for you." As I listened, for the first time in my inner being, I knew that I had a problem in my relationship with God. My sins separated me from Him. That was a revelation from the Holy Spirit.

The answer to my problem was that if I trusted Jesus Christ, in His death as payment for my sins and in His resurrection from the dead, God would forgive me. Well, that sounded like a pretty good deal. I could be forgiven by just trusting in Jesus.

Looking back, I paint the following figurative picture of that event. It was as if I walked up to the gate named "salvation." But I was clothed with all the externals that I wore to give my life meaning—my peers, my activities, and so forth. None of that clothing, however—none of my externals—could get me through that gate. None of them could address the inner need I felt. I had to shed those clothes if I wanted to get through the gate, because the gate wasn't wide enough for both me and the clothes. I had to stop trusting in my externals and put my trust only in Christ. So I took off those clothes, my externals, and went through the gate naked, because I had nothing to offer God but me.

Walking through that first gate was like putting on a new pair of jeans. I got the vital parts covered. I got my sins forgiven. For the first time I didn't just have externals in my life. I had a true inner identity: I was saved and I was forgiven. But that was all I knew about my new identity. That was good—very good—but the new jeans weren't enough to clothe all of me. Being forgiven was great, but I needed more than that to give my life meaning. I thought I still needed more clothes to cover me up, something else to make my life whole.

So I reached for some new externals to add to my wardrobe. I received Christ in a Baptist church, so I put on the identity of "Baptist." I began to run around and find out what Baptists believed, what we stood for, and how to conduct my life properly. It was exciting. It's fun when you have a brand-new external, like a kid at Christmas who has a new toy. But it doesn't take long to get tired of a new toy, does it?

I went to a Baptist college, which I enjoyed. I was learning about the Word of God. I progressed to seminary, but it wasn't as much fun there. I began to spend more time in the gym than in the library, but I studied enough to get through. And now I had a new external identity.

"Who are you?"

"I'm Pastor Stone."

"What are you?"

"I'm a Baptist."

Before, I just had new jeans. Now, I had some more new clothes. My new robes were called "Baptist." You've had your own new robes, haven't you? They may have been your job, your church, your family, your activities, your performance—any external you seek life from.

At this point I did have some internal reality—the jeans God had clothed me with. It's a revelation from God to know that Jesus Christ is more than a man, that He's the Son of God, the Savior of the world. It's a revelation to know your sins are forgiven. But I still had a whole lot of externals from which I was seeking more life: my denomination, my vocation, my performance. Those were the new clothes I had found for myself. Unfortunately, knowing that I was saved and that my sins were forgiven was the only inner reality I knew. Like most Christians, I was trying to live the Christian life on that raw reality.

The trouble is that, as true as it is, having your sins forgiven doesn't tell you one thing about how to live the life. The only thing it says is after you commit a sin, you are forgiven. You don't know anything yet about true life—God's life. So life to you is still external. You ask: "How do I do it? Give me a plan, give me a method, give me a scheme."

It's as if the day we receive Him by faith, Jesus says, "Now you're saved. Good luck. I'll see you when you die and it will be wonderful. But in the here and now it's up to you. Get out there and try as hard as you can."

What a struggle! I tried as hard as I could for years. After God had given me enough misery trying to be a good Baptist, I got to the point where I thought, "I've done all of these Baptist things. I've kept their Golden Rules. I've kept their commandments. Now where is the life?"

We move from outer to inner—from seeking life through externals to drawing life from the internal One—by letting the outer become exhausted. We let the outer do what it can do, because for a while the outer is fun and exciting. It's life to us, until it becomes routine and we have to keep performing to measure up. Finally, though, we say, "There's got to be something more." And there is something more. We are meant to get to the internal, and we can't be content until we get there. We can be momentarily satisfied with a new toy, but we can't be permanently content until we get to the place that God means to get us.

So we drag up near the next gate, exhausted by our own self-effort to live the Christian life. We're pleading, "Where's the life?"

The Holy Spirit says to us, "Yes, there's more."

"Where is it?" we ask.

"Over here."

"Good, I want to come."

We run up to the gate, but we bump into it and bounce back, because we can't get through. We still have our own robes on, the externals we are trusting to give us life. The robes, although tattered and torn by now, are too thick to get through the gate. The only way to get through that gate is to take off those externals again. We will never get through a new gate as long as we base our identity and meaning on outer things, whatever they may be.

I approached my second gate in my midthirties. I was lying on my bed of affliction, which is called depression. My outer identity, being a Baptist preacher, didn't satisfy me anymore, and I didn't know where to turn. At home in my bed, I had the shades down and the curtains drawn over the shades, and the room still wasn't dark enough for me. So I was under the covers, because I was trying to get the room as dark as I was. Some friends called, though, and asked me to lead a retreat. There's one thing a Baptist preacher can't resist: an invitation to speak. I don't care if he's on oxygen, he'll manage to preach. So I said, "I'll be there." Most of the people at the retreat were from my hometown church, but I hadn't seen them in twelve years.

I still hadn't moved beyond my first gate. I was primarily preaching salvation: how to receive Christ. I was talking about many different things, but all I truly knew was salvation.

I was supposed to be teaching these folks, but I was watching them and, to my surprise, they were teaching me. These weren't the same people I had left twelve years before. God had been moving on in them, but He hadn't gone any farther in me yet. I called Barbara, my wife, and told her, "Something's happened to our friends. They're different."

I'm like you. I have a heart for God, just like you do. If we sense something is real and we are hungry, we want it. Whatever my friends had, I wanted it.

At that time, the extent of my inner knowing was Christ died *for* me. My friends' inner knowing was Christ is *with* me and He's in me to help me. That was farther down the pike than I was, so I thought, *This is the next thing to come along for me; I'm going to grab it.*

That was my next gate, my next point of shedding more externals and experiencing more of God's inner life. To make it through the gate, though, I had to take off all the extra robes, all the externals I had clothed myself with. In my case, I had to shed my denominational robes that I had been trusting to provide me life. I could go through only with my new jeans, the one internal reality that God Himself had clothed me with: the fact that my sins were forgiven. So I walked through that next gate, and it led me into what we called the charismatic renewal.

Going through that next gate is like God putting a T-shirt over your jeans. Your inner knowing of God's life is expanded. I knew more about the inner life than I had known before the first gate. I knew more of the Spirit of God in me.

But I still had some bare spots I thought I needed to cover up. So once again I reached for some externals to clothe myself with. I ran out and learned what it was to be a charismatic. And I wondered about my old denominational friends: *How can those folks stay in those dead churches? This is the most exciting thing around. This is where the life is.*

For a while, life was great. During the praise services I was emotionally high and stimulated. But I confused those feelings of happiness with God's inner joy. I was looking for a permanent high, and I stayed on a high for about six months. I had to attend a lot of meetings to stay up there. I had to stand on my feet a long time and sing an awful lot of songs. Everybody did.

If we would be honest with ourselves, however, most of us were still searching. So much of our activity still involved externals. We were still desperate. We went to those meetings to get something. I went to get blessed, get healed, get delivered. Everybody went with a great need. But we'd leave, stepping right outside those doors, and we still had that need. Deep down we were still saying, "Where's the life?"

During this time we were part of a little prayer group that included a lady much younger than I. I loved my wife, Barbara, but I began feeling very enamored with this young lady. And I was confused, because the message I was hearing (I'm not saying this was actually being taught) was, "If you're high, it's the Holy Spirit. If you're emotionally worked up, if you're excited, if you feel good, it's the Holy Spirit." Here I was having good feelings about this young lady, but I knew those good feelings couldn't be the Holy Spirit. It was eating me up inside.

This time, though, I didn't get depressed. I got angry. I had put 21 years into this Jesus thing. I'd gone everywhere I'd heard that there was life. I had listened to everybody I could. And I had reached a bottomless pit. At that point I wrote my letter of resignation. I told God I was checking out.

Twenty-one years of trying to live for Jesus. I had known Christ for me. I had known Christ with me. I had begun to experience the concept of Christ in me, but I hadn't yet experienced Christ as me, expressing His life *as me*. Rather, it was Christ in me to help *me* become something. To make something out of *me*. And I had come to my end.

Over the years, I had gradually concluded that I couldn't pull off living the Christian life. I was a failure at it. But in one area I seemed like a success. Barbara said what a good husband I was. Yet here I was as her husband having feelings for this younger woman, and it was not good. I saw that, regardless of how much I loved God, given the right circumstances I was capable of anything. Trying to live in my own strength for God, or even trying to live with His help, I was still a dangerous creature in this world. It was the love of God to show me that I couldn't live the Christian life no matter how hard I tried.

It was about this time Barbara asked me to read a book called *Power in Praise*. I had already told her, "Barbara, I'm through with the Christian thing. I know that when I die, I'm going to heaven, but I'm through with this charade." It was spring and I was sitting in the yard under the trees, pouting. I was so far back in the doghouse with her that I thought if reading a book would help me get out, I'd read it.

So I did. And God had one thing for me in that book, a passage of Scripture: "In everything give thanks; for this is God's will for you in Christ Jesus" (1 Thessalonians 5:18).

I didn't give thanks for the ugly things. Do you? I thought, *You really don't give thanks in* everything. *You give thanks for the* good *things.* But that isn't what the Bible said. And though my soul was pouting and angry with God, that word became spirit and life to me. So I began to say, "Thank You, God. I'm still just as mad as I can be, but I'm being obedient. So, thank You. I'm still grinding my teeth so much that I'm lucky to have any enamel left, but thank You. I don't understand it, and I'm not particularly happy about it, but thank You."

It's odd, but I began to get some insight into what was going on. I saw that God had to kill me off in that area where I thought I was good, so that He could honor a prayer I had always prayed: "I want to be Your man." Just like you might have prayed, "I want to be Your man." "I want to be Your woman." Then you see that it's the love of God to crucify your own sense of goodness. While everybody else is saying, "He's fallen," God just sees the vessel that He's making.

The insight God provided finally led me to say concerning my most recent gate, "You know, this has been wonderful. I've learned a lot here, but I don't have the final answer. For me, there's got to be more. Where's the life?"

At that point the Holy Spirit said to me, in essence, "There is more, Dan, but you have to take off that external you have."

"Again? What is my external now, Lord?"

"You have to take off that charismatic external. If you want Me, you can't have any externals."

I took off those outer robes again. I've discovered that when the time comes you're about ready to shed whatever you need to, like some old dirty clothes. So there I stood, with only the inner, spirit realities that God had revealed to me: my jeans and my T-shirt. With those, I was able to get through my next gate, which was *Christ in you, the hope of glory.*

A lady had invited Barbara to hear a speaker, Norman Grubb. After the meeting Barbara asked him, "Would you come to my house and talk to my husband? He needs to hear what you said."

Months later, Norman came and spoke to a small group in our living room. The first thing he said was, "You can't live the Christian life."

I thought, *Amen to that. I am a walking testimony to that. You can't live the Christian life.*

Then he said, "Christ is the life."

Well, I knew that. I had a head knowledge of that.

But finally he stated, "Christ is in you and He will live the life."

And my spirit responded, *Ohhhh! It's not "He will help me live the life," but "He will live the life." That's the good news! I can let Him live the life.*

I had 21 years of trying on my own. I was absolutely convinced I couldn't live the Christian life, not the way the Bible described it. Now I realized, *Christ can. I'll let Him live it in me.* It was a revelation from the Holy Spirit.

In the following days God added to that inner revelation. He put His clothing on me. I had too many exposed spots that I had tried to cover up with externals. He put His whole wardrobe on me. In truth, His clothes had been on me all along. I just didn't know it.

For the first time I came to know that He had already made me the righteousness of God in Christ (2 Corinthians 5:21). I was truly righteous. He had made me holy (Colossians 3:12). He had made me complete (Colossians 2:10). I was blameless in His sight (Colossians 1:22). And loved. And acceptable.

The Lord taught me that when I was crucified on the cross with Christ, as Galatians 2:20 had told me for so long, I died to myself as my point of reference. He living in me was my point of reference. He would live His life through me, as me. Has He revealed that to you? If He hasn't, He wants to, because that's the truly good news.

We have only two basic questions in life: how do I get my sins forgiven, and how do I live the life? We may have found out how to get our sins forgiven, but most of us haven't yet discovered how to live the life. You can't. That's the first thing you have to learn. *He* can. And, He will. He will live His life in us, as us.

You have to go through those gates, though. You have to lay down the externals that you have tried to draw life from.

When you finally go through the last gate, it's like the Old Testament priest going into the Holy of Holies. He was in there with just one Person—God. Everything else was external. It was just him and God.

After receiving Christ, in your awareness you have a little internal, a lot of external. You go through more gates and you have a little more internal, still some external. In the end, God brings you to your Holy of Holies, to live in your spirit. You live as an internal person. No more trusting the externals.

When you have entered into that "knowing" in your inner being, no external can tell you anything about yourself. Your identity and your life come from God. When I used to speak to groups, Barbara would remind me, "Tell them about my gate." She found out that she had an external. It was me. She was Dan's wife. I was her sufficiency. I was her adequacy. I was her identity. One night she had to go out and lie on a blanket under the stars and do business with God. He said, "You have an idol in your life. It's your husband." After that night, I was no longer Barbara's god.

We all have different robes we have to shed. Some people have robes called children. For others, it's a profession, or possessions, or addictions, or a finely cultivated image. Many Christians have a robe called "ministry." Anything that's external, that's telling you something about yourself,

God has to take it to the altar and kill it so He can be your all in all. When you see that, you praise God for it.

We have to be grateful to God because He drives us to Himself. But He does it with love. He says to us, "You want that, you can have it. You want that external, go get it. I know you're going to lay it down. I'm not going to keep you from picking it up, touching it, examining it, playing with it awhile, and finally putting it down. Then you'll pick up and put down the next thing, and the next thing, and the next. One day you're going to get to the final gate. You're going to walk into that holy place and you're going to meet Me. Not that you haven't met Me before, but you're going to meet Me and Me only, and you'll have the answer."

"Good Teacher, where is the life?"

"Well, you've been religious."

"Yes, Lord, I've done the denominational thing."

"Well, you tried the other religious route."

"Yes, Lord, I've been charismatic."

"And you've done the success thing."

"Yes, Lord, I have, but where is the life?"

When you are perfectly prepared, Jesus whispers the old news, which is still the good news: "I am the life. You take Me into you, and you have the life. I live the life as you, just as the Father revealed His life as Me."

Then the 21 years in the wilderness turn into a blessing. The lost job yields a blessing. The wayward child becomes a blessing. The failed marriage reveals a blessing. You've gone through those gifts of misery and you thank God for them, because you came out with one precious possession: Him. You've come to the end—He in you and you in Him. You have arrived at the pearl of great price. There isn't anyplace else to go.

Where is the life? "The gate is small and the way is narrow that leads to life." May this book be a beacon to you, shining on that final gate, pointing the way to the only One who is true life.

2

The Line

God spoke to me numerous times through my wife, Barbara. One day she asked me, "What would you do if you could do anything you wanted to? And don't stop to think about your answer."

I said, "I'd like to leave my current job and go tell Baptists, our people, who they are in Christ, because they don't know." That was a broad statement, but it's generally true. Most Christians don't know.

She answered, "Okay, let's do it."

That was God.

I left my job and we started traveling around the country, meeting with small groups, sharing what God had made a reality in our lives. The first thing I always shared was something I call "The Line." I started with it because the line clarifies vital truth in a way that's easy to grasp. Much of what follows in this book has its foundation in this simple teaching tool based on 2 Corinthians 4:18:

> ...we look not at the things which are *seen*, but at the things
> which are *not seen*; for the things which are seen are *temporal*,
> but the things which are not seen are *eternal*.

That verse contains two truths. One truth talks about things that are seen and temporal, or temporary. The other truth talks about things that are unseen and eternal. I simply draw a line that separates the two.

Above the line is the unseen and eternal; below the line is the seen and temporal, or temporary.

ETERNAL
Unseen

Seen
TEMPORAL

Of course, there's really no such thing as a line. These two realms coexist. The unseen and eternal is going on in the midst of the seen and temporal. As believers, we have the privilege of living an unseen and eternal life in the midst of this seen and temporal world. Because we think in concepts, however, it helps to separate these two realities with the line to understand them better.

As 2 Corinthians 4:18 indicates, the realm above the line is invisible and eternal. It is changeless and timeless. It is the realm of spirit and of God's absolutes. It is the realm of ultimate reality, of the uncreated, of completeness and wholeness, where things are finished and settled. The eternal realm can be illustrated by the word *now*. It's the realm of God's I AM, where things simply *are*.

The realm below the line is visible and temporary. We call it the natural realm. The apostle Paul calls it "this age." It is the created realm of matter and appearances. It has a beginning and an end. It is the realm of past, present, and future; birth, life, and death; sowing, growing, and reaping. It's a realm of activity, process, and need. It's a realm where we often say, "I want to grow in Christ." It's a realm in which we see both good and evil. Whereas the unseen and eternal is the realm of "I am," the seen and temporal is the realm of "I am becoming."

Spirit	"I AM"	Ultimate Reality
Wholeness	**ETERNAL**	Changeless
Complete	Unseen	Timeless
In Process	Seen	Time-based
Need	**TEMPORAL**	Changing
Matter	"I am becoming"	Appearances

We're not talking here about a Greek dualism or gnosticism in which one realm, spirit, is pure and all-important, and another realm, matter, is unclean and unimportant or even unreal. Both realms are vitally important to God, because He has made both of them. The seen and temporal is a true realm and is important. We live in the seen and temporal realm. But we are simply acknowledging what Paul says, that there are two realms and that one is greater than the other. We are to focus on the eternal realm.

Many Scripture verses illustrate the difference between the two realms. When Moses asked God His name, God replied, "I AM WHO I AM" (Exodus 3:14). He told Moses to tell the Hebrews that "I AM" had sent him. God's very name indicates the changeless, timeless, eternal, present-tense nature of His being. Jesus used the same language to refer to Himself: "Truly, truly, I say to you, before Abraham was born, I am" (John 8:58). The writer to the Hebrews stated: "Jesus Christ is the same yesterday and today and forever" (13:8). God is the unseen, eternal, timeless, changeless One.

At the appointed time, however, I AM went below the line and entered the seen and temporal realm He had created. "And the Word became flesh, and dwelt among us" (John 1:14). The changeless, timeless One became a seen and temporal man.

As a man, Jesus experienced all that we experience below the line. He had a past, a present, and a future. He experienced growth, both as a child (Luke 2:40) and as an adult (Hebrews 5:8). He had needs, just as any person has.

In a similar way, we as God's children live both above the line and below the line. The verse that best illustrates this is Hebrews 10:14: "For by one offering He has perfected forever those who are being sanctified" (NKJV).

God has already perfected those of us who are in Christ. We are complete in Him (Colossians 2:10). We are His righteousness (2 Corinthians 5:21). We are holy and blameless and beyond reproach (Colossians 1:22). These truths are already our reality above the line, in the unseen and eternal realm, in God's kingdom, in our spirit. These are the eternal, unchanging truths of our identity as new creations, as sons and daughters whom God has birthed (John 3:3-6).

Below the line, however, in the seen and temporal realm, we're in the process of being sanctified. We have needs. Our emotions fluctuate. Our behavior changes. We experience growth.

The distinction between these two realms is vital to us for three reasons. First, in the here and now, God has designed His kingdom to work by faith. God could have placed the eternal in the visible realm. His eternal kingdom would then be plainly seen. But if He had done that, there wouldn't be any faith. Everything would be exactly as it appears to be, and faith would be pointless.

But the whole universe operates on faith. We, in particular, were designed to operate by faith. We have the privilege of looking through the seen and temporal to the unseen and eternal. By the Spirit of God we discern what, from God's perspective, is taking place in the seen and the temporal around us.

That's how Jesus lived. He saw the seen and temporal around Him, but when the man stretched out his withered hand, Jesus didn't see the withered hand as ultimate. When they brought Jesus five loaves and two fish, He didn't see that insufficiency as ultimate. When they took Him to the dead girl, He didn't see that death as ultimate.

In each case Jesus saw beyond the outward appearance to what His Father was doing. He lived in another realm. He invites you and me to do the same.

Second, the distinction is important because it enables us to understand our true identity in Christ. As believers, our failures, sins, and shortcomings—all below-the-line realities—constantly confront us. Unless we understand that our true, eternal identity lies above the line in our spirit (the identity God gave us at our new birth), we will habitually draw our identity from our below-the-line performance, whether good or bad. Our focus will be on trying to clean up our act and look good enough for God to accept.

That's where almost all Christians are living: trying to become something they already are. We have it backward. In God's economy, in the seen realm we become because in the unseen realm we already are. As we know and rest in the unseen and eternal realm, God manifests its truth in the visible realm. "For by one offering He has perfected forever those who are being sanctified." In the unseen, eternal realm, God has already perfected us. In the seen and temporal realm, God is bringing that perfection, or completion, into view.

That's why we can say we are complete and a new creation while simultaneously, in the seen and temporal realm, a process is going on. From God's point of view, in the unseen and eternal realm, we are a finished product. In the seen and temporal, He is continuing to work the truth deeper into us and conform us to His image.

Third, the distinction between the two realms is important because God has designed us so that we can find fulfillment only in the unseen and eternal realm. The seen and temporal realm offers many pleasures that God has provided, but none of them ultimately satisfy. That's why Jesus said, "I am the bread of life; he who comes to Me will not hunger, and he who believes in Me will never thirst" (John 6:35). There isn't anything below the line, no matter how beautiful, no matter how touching, no matter how true, that equals life. We find true life only above the line, in God. *He* is life.

God has created each of us with a thirst that only He can quench. French philosopher Pascal called it a God-shaped vacuum in our hearts that only He can fill. Or as Augustine put it, "Our souls are restless until they find their rest in Thee." Man is perpetually seeking. To whatever degree we don't know the unseen and eternal realm, we seek answers in the seen and temporal. We look for eternal answers among temporal things. But we discover they can't provide them.

We are programmed for failure if we're looking for ultimate answers in a nonultimate realm, a realm that's partial, fragmented, incomplete. We end up worshipping the creation rather than the Creator. We can do that as believers. The total answer is a Person, Jesus Christ. It's part of God's program to make us dissatisfied with what the temporal realm offers so that we might seek life in Him.

A life of faith, our true identity, and our fulfillment in life are all based in the unseen and eternal realm. Our problem is that we can't see that realm or learn of it through empirical investigation. Presently, God's unseen and eternal kingdom is within us, but we can understand the things of that realm only if God reveals them to us:

> For to us God revealed them through the Spirit...Now we
> have received, not the spirit of the world, but the Spirit who
> is from God, so that we may know the things freely given to
> us by God...(1 Corinthians 2:10,12).

We are completely dependent on the Holy Spirit to be our teacher. To whatever degree the Holy Spirit has revealed to us the unseen and eternal realm, we live in it. To whatever degree we do not understand by revelation the unseen and eternal realm of God's kingdom, we're locked into living in the seen and temporal realm.

God makes known to us the eternal, unseen, spirit realities of His own domain by revelation. He breaks through into our consciousness and reveals eternal truths not discernible in the realm of appearances. And we respond, "Oh, I see!"

At that moment, revelation has met with faith on our part, and when revelation encounters faith, it produces an inner knowing. This happens to us progressively.

One of our first revelations is that Jesus Christ is the Son of God and the Savior of the world. The natural (unsaved) man doesn't know that. He cannot know it, even if he hears it over and over. Only the Holy Spirit can reveal to Him the reality of Jesus Christ (1 Corinthians 2:14).

Once we place our faith in Christ, the next revelation is that our sins are forgiven. That is an unseen and eternal truth. Nothing in the seen and temporal tells us that. The Holy Spirit reveals it. As I said in chapter 1, I lived primarily on that revelation for 21 years. But God continues to reveal unseen and eternal truths to us that expand our spiritual understanding.

As believers, you and I live below the line, but we aren't really below-the-line people. We are of God's kingdom. But we live in a realm of temporal appearances that differ from what God sees in the unseen and eternal. Spiritual growth is a process of replacing temporal appearances with eternal reality, and living out of it.

As you know inner life—the life of the Spirit—you can't help but live it. Generally, except for brief excursions, we're always living out what we believe. We can't escape that. We don't do anything but live what we believe. As we understand the unseen and eternal realm, we live it, and as we live it, we become less and less oriented toward the seen and temporal. It exercises less control over us.

For example, Paul tells us in Romans 6 that we died to sin and are free from it. That is an unseen and eternal truth (about which I will say more later). Sin no longer has any power over us. But if we don't know that unseen and eternal truth, sin still exercises power over us. That's because we're caught in the trap of trying to become something we already are: free from sin.

We will never know abundant life until the unseen and eternal realm is home to us in our everyday experience. Until then, we will live according to appearances, and appearances will never lead us deeper into the life of God. Only faith will.

God wants to bring us to the point where we say, "I live by what God says about the things in my life—situations, people, and myself." Then we see as He sees. We discern that situations aren't as they appear to be, but that God's absolutes are operating in the realm of appearances. We are at rest in the unseen and eternal realm, and we experience His fullness within us.

In our daily lives as believers, the most important thing we can know from the unseen and eternal realm is that we and God are one, or in union. That sounds heretical, but that is exactly what the Bible says:

> But he who is joined to the Lord is one spirit with Him
> (1 Corinthians 6:17, NKJV).

God has permanently joined Himself to your spirit. Your spirit and He are one. The two operate as one unit. When we begin to know and live out of that truth, all the promises of the New Testament suddenly cease to be pie in the sky. They become daily realities. We understand that there is no more separation—God up there and us down here. We cease striving to get closer to God. We stop asking, "How do I reach Him? Give me the programs, give me the plans, give me the ways." Instead, we live out of what is already true. We live in union. God and you are one. In the seen and temporal, He operates as you. You rest in Him.

Every one of us who has believed in Christ is complete in Christ (Colossians 2:10). We are already holy (Colossians 3:12). We are already perfect (Hebrews 10:14). We are His righteousness (2 Corinthians 5:21). There's nothing else to be done. As we see that, we will live that, and God will make what is already true in the unseen and eternal a seen and temporal experience.

In chapter 3, we will see what God did in the unseen and eternal realm to make our union with Him an already-accomplished truth and His rest an available reality.

3

Doublecross, Part One:
You Died in Christ

Several years ago I was invited back to preach at the first church I pastored after I left seminary. I had pastored that church two decades earlier; now they had asked me to preach on their two-hundredth anniversary.

So I returned and said to them, "Beloved, when I was your pastor, I only gave you fifty percent of the gospel. I have come back today to share the other fifty percent with you. Not only did Christ die for our sins, but He is our indwelling life. He has come to be the life that is impossible for us to become."

The vast majority of believers know only half of the gospel. The first 12 years I pastored, *I* knew only half of the gospel. I preached a steady diet of "Christ died for the forgiveness of your sins." Week after week I gave the same basic message. The problem was that my audience had already been saved; their sins had already been forgiven.

The only other message I had to offer was telling them what they ought to be doing: external compliance with commandments. I was handing out my own version of legalism. They listened, of course. Their hearts were like mine: they wanted to serve God, to do the right thing. So we would accept those ought-tos and try to do them.

But all during that time I was thinking, *There's got to be more. We're not getting anywhere. We're just rehearsing the same message Sunday after Sunday. I'm not growing; the people aren't growing. We're putting a lot of effort into it, but we're really not going anywhere spiritually.*

Why weren't we getting anywhere? Because one half of the gospel isn't enough.

Let me illustrate the half we knew. Imagine we are transported back in time to Jerusalem almost 2000 years ago. We hear that the Roman authorities are having a crucifixion that day. So, like everybody else, we go out to see the event. And what do we see? Two thieves and someone accused of being a political rabble-rouser, an enemy of Caesar. That's what we see in the seen and temporal realm.

So we watch, and in the middle of the afternoon the man in the middle dies. Being Americans, we can't stay riveted to anything too long, so we wonder, "What else is going on in town?"

But then something odd happens. It's like a voice within us says, "That wasn't a political rabble-rouser. That was My Son. I'm God the Father. That was God the Son. And He died for your sins. If you will receive that, your sins will be forgiven."

We hear that and respond, "I'll accept that. God is offering me the forgiveness of my sins. I'll receive that from Him."

All of us who have believed in Christ have had that experience. It isn't important that you know the day or the time it happened, but it's important that you know it has happened so that you can say, "I know that my sins have been forgiven." That's a revelation from the Holy Spirit. Nothing in the seen and temporal realm tells you that your sins have been forgiven. That's an unseen and eternal truth that the Holy Spirit reveals to you.

I call this the first side of the cross: Christ died for you. The message that "Christ died for our sins" (1 Corinthians 15:3) is spread throughout the New Testament:

> In Him we have redemption through His blood, the forgiveness of our trespasses, according to the riches of His grace, which He lavished on us (Ephesians 1:7-8).

> For He rescued us from the domain of darkness, and transferred us to the kingdom of His beloved Son, in whom we have redemption, the forgiveness of sins (Colossians 1:13-14).

> When you were dead in your transgressions and the uncircumcision of your flesh, He made you alive together with Him, having forgiven us all our transgressions (Colossians 2:13).

> He Himself is the propitiation [satisfaction] for our sins (1 John 2:2).

It's a thrilling thing to have your sins forgiven. Just knowing that we are forgiven and have right standing with God is usually enough to carry us for many months after our salvation as we revel in God's amazing grace toward us.

Soon, however, we encounter a problem. Because the Holy Spirit can teach us only one thing from this event in Jerusalem of Christ dying for us: "Your sins are forgiven." That's the basic truth that event contains. But once we are forgiven, we have to start living the life. And we ask, "How do I live this thing out? How do I get my act together? How do I keep from sinning? How do I make it work?"

What we discover is that the truth that we're forgiven doesn't tell us one thing about how to live the life. It only addresses the question, "What do I do about my sins?" It has nothing to do with living the life. But forgiveness is the only inner revelation we have so far from the Holy Spirit. We don't have any revelation on how to live the life. So we take this one revelation, that our sins are forgiven, and try to stretch it to somehow cover how to live the life.

You know how we do that. We go out and try to live the Christian life, but we can't quite pull it off. Instead, we sin a little bit (or a lot) and then we get forgiven before we go to bed that night. Or we get forgiven on Sunday at church. As a preacher, I took my congregation through that every Sunday: "We have sins of commission; we have sins of omission. Surely you've done something wrong this week. Now let's ask God to forgive us."

Isn't that the way it is, either at church or for us individually? There's no way out of that because we don't have anything from the Lord yet on how to live the life. So our preoccupation is with whom? Ourselves. And our sins. We're still seeing ourselves externally, based on our performance. And we're on a roller coaster because our performance goes up and down and we never can measure up. So we're very unhappy, but we smile—a fake smile. We go to church and say, "I'm fine. Are you fine? I'm fine too." We think, *I'm actually miserable, but it's Sunday and I can't say I'm miserable in church because everybody is "happy." Happy, happy. Where's the coffee? I need more Spirit. More caffeine.*

That's the way it is.

After you get over the thrill of being saved, you're stuck on this treadmill. It's worse than being lost. I don't mean it's actually worse than being lost, but it feels like it. Because when you were lost, you were comfortably lost. I always say, you don't have to do anything to be lost; you just get up and put on your britches. I never read a book on how to be lost. It was my nature to be lost. You're always comfortable with your nature. You're comfortable walking around on two feet. You're not quite as comfortable if you drop down on your knees and spend the whole day crawling. It's not our nature to crawl. We were comfortable being lost because that used to be our nature.

It's easier to be lost than to be saved and try to live only off "I'm forgiven," striving your utmost to be a good Christian. Because that isn't the whole gospel. That isn't the whole gospel! It is only a partial, fragmentary view of our salvation. So we have 50 percent of the gospel, and then we go back into the flesh, into our independent self-effort, trying to make the rest of it happen on our own.

We can't make it happen, however, which is according to the program. We're programmed for failure when we try to make the Christian life work on our own. This kind of living will bring us to despair. It produces nothing but an inner sense of condemnation.

Many people finally conclude that's how the Christian life is supposed to be. I've actually heard ministers tell their congregations that truly victorious living is impossible and that the Christian life is nothing but a struggle in which you are going to experience defeat after defeat. That's a far cry from the "abundant life" Jesus promised.

Why this discrepancy? Because the first half of the cross deals only with the issue of sins. S-I-N-S. Plural. Because Christ died on the cross, our S-I-N-S are forgiven. God has wiped the slate clean of all the offenses we have or ever will commit against Him.

Getting our sins forgiven, though, doesn't deal with the question of sin. S-I-N. Singular. Sins are the product of something the Bible says dwells within us—sin (Romans 7:17).

Sin is a power or force that is in rebellion against God and produces sins as its fruit. We inherited sin through Adam, from whom sin was passed to every subsequent generation (Romans 5:12). As long as sin dwells in the center of our being, it will produce sins. We can get those sins forgiven, but that doesn't take care of the source of the sins. So we're on the treadmill: we sin, we get forgiven; we sin, we get forgiven. Over and over and over.

We read the Bible, though, and think that one day sin won't dog us anymore, causing us to do what we don't want to do. We see God's promises about how abundant life is supposed to be and how we have victory over sin. But because we don't experience God's promises in the here and now, we conclude that an event must take place before we can experience them. That event is: we must die.

We tell ourselves that once we physically die we're going to move into the unseen and eternal realm. Then we're going to have everything that we've anticipated. So we push all of God's promises off into the eternal future, and we say, "This whole struggle isn't going to end until I die. When I die, I'm going to join the unseen and eternal realm, and everything is going to be great."

There came a time in my life, however, when I read those promises and realized that none of them applied to the future. Every one of them was supposed to apply to my life now. "For as many as are the promises of God, in Him they are yes" (2 Corinthians 1:20). Not *will be* yes. *Are* yes. God didn't intend me to relegate them to His divine eternity. He meant for Dan Stone to experience them *now*.

I had been right about one thing. I had concluded that the only way for me to experience these promises was to die. When I died, I'd finally be free from me. That's the absolute truth. We all have to die to enter into these unseen and eternal realities. So I always say to people, "Yes, you do have to die, but the real issue is *when* did you die?" I found out that I died much earlier than I ever thought. Here I was waiting for something to happen that in the unseen and eternal realm had already happened to me.

Let's go back to our illustration 2000 years ago. We were standing outside Jerusalem observing a crucifixion. Previously, the Holy Spirit told us that the center man was God's Son, and He died for the forgiveness of our sins. But now the illustration changes. Suddenly we are transported off the ground and up into the body of Christ Himself. We are no longer observers of something He is doing for us. We are participating with Him in the event. We are being crucified with Him. And when He dies, we die with Him. This is exactly what Paul explained in Romans 6:

> Do you not know that all of us who have been baptized into Christ Jesus have been baptized into His death? Therefore we have been buried with Him through baptism into death, so that as Christ was raised from the dead through the glory of the Father, so we too might walk in newness of life. For if we have become united with Him in the likeness of His death, certainly we shall also be in the likeness of His resurrection, knowing this, that our old [man] was crucified with Him, in order that our body of sin might be done away with, so that we would no longer be slaves to sin; for he who has died is freed from sin (6:3-7).

I used to read that passage wrongly. Being Baptist, when I came across the word *baptized* all I could see was a pool of water. But the Greek word *baptizo* didn't mean what baptize means to us. It simply meant to immerse or to place into. Rather than translate it into the English word *immerse*, Bible translators just turned the Greek word into an English word. *Baptizo* became *baptize*. And whenever someone says baptize, we think of water and a religious ceremony.

But we get a clearer meaning when we simply translate it directly into the corresponding English word: "Don't you know that all of us who have been immersed into Christ Jesus have been immersed into His death?" Water isn't there. Paul is saying that we were immersed in Christ. We went into Him. He swallowed us up.

"All of us who have been immersed into Christ Jesus have been immersed into His death." Why? Because He died. And whatever happened to Jesus on the cross happened to whoever was immersed in Him. We were all immersed into Him. We were in Him on that cross, experiencing what He experienced. So when He died, we died. When He was raised, we were raised with Him. To emphasize the point, Paul said that we were "buried with Him." When you bury somebody, what does it mean? They are dead. The human life is over. Whatever they were is gone.

The question that confronts us is this: What died with Christ? It certainly doesn't seem like I died with Him. Here I am, still alive and well in Kentucky. Jesus died 2000 years ago in Jerusalem. How could I have possibly died with Him?

The answer is found in Romans 6:6: "knowing this, that our old [man] was crucified with Him." Your old man—the one you inherited from Adam, cut off from God but alive to the power of sin—was crucified with Christ. Ephesians 2:1-3 describes the life that flowed from the old man:

> And you were dead in your trespasses and sins, in which you formerly walked according to the course of this world, according to the prince of the power of the air [Satan], of the spirit that is now working in the sons of disobedience. Among them we too all formerly lived in the lusts of our flesh, indulging the desires of the flesh and of the mind, and were by nature children of wrath, even as the rest.

The source of that life had to die. You can't put Band-Aids on it. It had to die. It had to be cut off. It's like the dandelions in the field next to my house. I used to break them off at the ground and hope for the best. But dandelion roots are very long. I didn't realize how long until I finally pulled one out. You have to get them out by the root or they'll grow right back. God had to cut off the old man at the root or he would continue to produce his sinful fruit. So God crucified you with Christ.

The old man is the human spirit indwelt by and enslaved to sin. But God crucified the old man and gave us a new spirit, created "in righteousness and holiness" (Ephesians 4:24). Hundreds of years before Christ, Ezekiel prophesied that God would do this under the New Covenant:

> "Moreover, I will give you a new heart and put a new spirit within you; and I will remove the heart of stone from your flesh and give you a heart of flesh. I will put My Spirit within you" (36:26-27a).

God removed our old human spirit, gave us a new human spirit, born of Him, and put His Spirit in us. In the depths of our being, we are completely new creatures. We were dead in trespasses and sins. But we are no longer. We were sons of disobedience. But we are no longer. We were expressing the desires of our spiritual father, Satan. But he is our father no longer. We were children of wrath. But we are no longer.

How could we have been crucified with Christ 2000 years ago? Because we weren't crucified physically, in the seen and temporal realm. We were crucified in the realm of spirit, the unseen and eternal realm. Remember the line? In the unseen and eternal realm, time has no meaning; everything is *now*.

That's why Jesus is the Lamb slain from before the foundation of the world. In the seen and temporal, He was the lamb slain 2000 years ago. In the unseen and eternal, He has always been the slain Lamb. In the seen and temporal realm, you and I live physically right now. In the unseen and eternal realm, you and I were crucified on the cross with Christ. Our old man, inherited from Adam, dead to and separated from God, died with Him.

This aspect of the cross—that we died with Him—is what I call the Doublecross. There are two sides of the cross. The first is the blood side. That's where Christ died for us. He shed His blood for the forgiveness of our sins. The second side is the body side. We were united with Him on the cross, participating in His death, burial, and resurrection. Our old man was crucified with Him. Our new man, righteous and holy, was resurrected with Him.

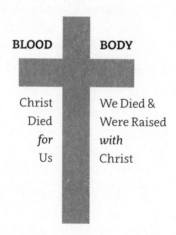

BLOOD   BODY

Christ Died *for* Us   We Died & Were Raised *with* Christ

These two sides of the cross are not unfamiliar to us. We celebrate them every time we take communion. We eat the bread. We drink the cup. Except most Christians don't have a clue as to what the bread, representing the body, really means. It means that we were united with Him and that when He died, we died. When He was buried, we were buried. When He was raised, we were raised. The heart of Paul's theology is built on the Lord's Supper: the blood and the body. Christ died for us; we died with Him.

We don't feel dead. We don't look dead. We often don't act dead. But at some point the Holy Spirit pulls back the curtain and shows us that in the deepest part of us, our spirit—who we truly are—a death has occurred that has forever changed us. We're going to look the same, feel the same, and think the same on many, many days. But we're going to know something: we're not the same.

In the unseen and eternal realm an exchange has taken place in our spirit that, once we know it, produces through us a quality of life that's different from anything else the world has seen. It's light in darkness. It's other-love in a world of self-love. It's desirable. And it's in us.

4

What You Died To

I used to meet occasionally with a small group of ladies to discuss our union with Christ. They would gather about 11:30 in the morning, open their little brown sack lunches, eat, and have Bible study. These ladies were what you might call elderly; most were in their eighties. I discovered that one of the problems with little ladies in their eighties is that after they have lunch, they want a nap. So if you have anything to say you'd better say it in a hurry, because they are going to start nodding off on you.

On one occasion, however, this 80-year-old lady wasn't about to nod off, she was so excited. I had just arrived when she ran up to me (she hadn't seen me in a year) and exclaimed, "I'm dead! I'm dead! I'm dead!"

I notice that as people get older their defenses often go down and they just say what's on their mind. Until then, we put on a facade of being nice. These little ladies had passed that point, though. One of them said, "We're so sick and tired of hearing her say that. That's all she does. She goes around saying, 'I'm dead! I'm dead! I'm dead!'"

I saw something for myself in that. If you had lived to be 80 and discovered that you had died in Christ, you'd be excited too. You're always going to talk about the latest good news, and her good news was: "I'm dead! I'm dead!" She hadn't died physically, of course, but she had died spiritually.

Previously she had been waiting to die physically to enjoy the goodies of the Lord. Now she was still physically alive but had entered into a new dimension with Christ as her life. She understood that she had died and was raised with Him.

In the last chapter we saw what I call the Doublecross: not only did Christ die for us (the blood side of the cross), but we also died with Him (the body side of the cross). We must know that our old man was crucified on the cross because our old man was the source of most of the problems we experience as humans.

Our old, unregenerate spirit, inherited from Adam, was by nature sinful. It was an enemy of God, separated from God, and without the life of God for which man was originally created. From the old man flowed sin, hatred, a sense of separation from God (and one another), and death.

For God to restore humanity to its original purpose, that old man had to die. Through His kindness, God accomplished that for us on the cross of Christ. In this chapter we will detail some of the benefits of the fact that our old man died. But before we do, we must establish this one fact: we all died with Christ. Paul tells us that repeatedly:

> For the love of Christ controls us, having concluded this, that one died for all, therefore all died (2 Corinthians 5:14).

> For you [plural] have died and your life is hidden with Christ in God (Colossians 3:3).

> Therefore, my brethren, you [plural] also were made to die... through the body of Christ (Romans 7:4).

> Or do you not know that all of us who have been baptized [immersed] into Christ Jesus have been baptized [immersed] into His death? (Romans 6:3).

That's incredible. It's something you can't entirely process through your brain. When one died, *all* died, because we were all in Him. That's not a seen and temporal statement, because humanity is stretched out over time from the beginning until today. The only realm in which this could happen is above the line, where there isn't any time. There everything is now. What we see as past, present, and future is simply now.

That all died in Christ is an unseen and eternal reality. It's just like when Adam sinned, all sinned. None were even born when Adam sinned, but all were in his loins. Likewise, all believers are "in the loins" of Christ.

It's easy for someone to say, "All died. That means all of you. But not me. I know me too well. I'm not dead yet."

That's the trap we can fall into: "It's true, but not for me."

But "all" means "all." And the beautiful thing is that all means all to God, whether all ever means all to us or not.

Even if we never see that we died spiritually until we physically die and then, looking back, see that the old us was dead, it doesn't change the reality: we were still already dead. God knows that. He already sees us differently than we see ourselves. We are inflicting punishment, guilt, and condemnation upon ourselves, day after day, episode after episode, for things about us that He isn't even seeing—because He can't see them. I don't mean He's blind. He can't see us that way because we're not that way to Him. So Paul could say about us:

> Therefore, if anyone is in Christ, he is a new creation; old things have passed away; behold, all things have become new. Now all things are of God, who has reconciled us to Himself through Jesus Christ (2 Corinthians 5:17-18a, NKJV).

That's good news. Previously, I was trying to get rid of the old and I was trying to make the new come. What a trap! In the unseen and eternal, Paul is telling us, "When Jesus died, you were in Him, and you died too. The old spirit is gone, the new spirit is come, and you are a new creation in Christ Jesus."

People have said to me, "I know that's my position in Christ, but it's not my condition." I don't like to use those words because they're not biblical and I find they mostly confuse people. What people mean is, "I know what you're telling me is true, but it's not my experience."

I reply, "Remember the line? Below the line things are temporal. Above the line things are eternal, and above the line is the greater truth. So your position is your true condition. In your spirit, you did die with Christ. You were raised with Him. You are holy and righteous and blameless. You may never evidence it in the seen and temporal, but God says you died, you were buried, you were raised, and you are seated in the heavenlies. The question you must ask yourself is, 'What am I going to agree is true? What God says or what I currently see?'"

Can you recognize that in the unseen and eternal, the realm of spirit, you've already died? When the Holy Spirit turns on the light and you say, "Oh, *now* I see!" you have become God's free person. You can stop wrestling with the flesh, trying to make it do things it could never do. You free yourself to be an expression of the indwelling Jesus Christ. You are the expression of Him in your own unique humanity.

When our old man died on the cross with Christ, there were certain things that we died *to*. Or to put it another way, our spirit ceased its relationship with certain things. These things no longer hold any power over us—over our spirit, our true identity. We are dead to them.

The first thing we died to is sin. Not sins, which are acts of unrighteousness, but sin, which is the power that produces those acts of unrighteousness.

In the last part of Romans 5, Paul talked about the riches of God's grace. But the apostle knew that as some people listened to his teaching on grace, they heard license. When the flesh hears pure grace teaching, it always hears license. The spirit praises God for His grace; the flesh hears license. So Paul knew that some were going to hear the good news and conclude, "I can do whatever I want and get away with it. I can do all the sinning I want to because I have all this grace of God to draw on and get all the forgiveness I want."

Well, that's true. Excuse me for taking the grace of God that far, but that's true. If you're really a born-again person, you can do whatever you want because God never sees what you used to be. He sees who you are now in Christ. But Paul responded, "God forbid that would be your conclusion. It's a truth, but God forbid you would conclude that." Or to use his own words:

> What shall we say then? Are we to continue in sin so that grace might increase? May it never be! How shall we who died to sin still live in it? (Romans 6:1-2).

Paul then immediately taught what we covered in the previous chapter: our union with Christ in His death, burial, and resurrection. Because we died with Christ, we are dead to sin. It no longer has any power over us.

> Knowing this, that our old [man] was crucified with Him, in
> order that our body of sin might be done away with, so that
> we would no longer be slaves to sin; for he who has died is
> freed from sin (Romans 6:6-7).

Years ago I saw that those who take advantage of the grace of God
and continue in sin—as well as those who are fearful of the full grace of
God—don't know something. They don't know they have died to sin.
They know they have been forgiven of sins, but they don't yet know they
have died to sin. There is no one in us, in our deepest being, our inner
man, that wants to sin.

I was speaking in Alabama to a group of 77 people. I asked them,
"How many of you believe the Bible?" All 77 hands went up. I read
Romans 6:7 to them: "He who has died is freed from sin." I continued,
"How many believe what I just read?" Three hands went up. "We've got
a problem here," I said. "You just said that you believe the Bible, and I
just read it to you." But they didn't really believe that. They didn't have a
spiritual awareness of being dead, buried, and risen with Christ.

The blood side of the cross deals with *sins*: actions or attitudes that
break the law of God. The body side of the cross deals with *sin*, whose
source was the old man, our old Adamic nature. He was the point of
origin of sins. God's solution to our dilemma was to become what our
problem was. But our problem wasn't our humanity, and it wasn't our
environment—our parents, the school we went to, which side of the
tracks we grew up on, or what we had or didn't have. Our problem
always was a spiritual problem: sin. Jesus didn't just identify with our
problem; He became the problem. "[God] made Him [Jesus] who knew
no sin to be sin on our behalf, so that we might become the righteousness of God in Him" (2 Corinthians 5:21). The cure was radical. Jesus
became sin and joined our old man to Himself. Thus, our old man died
with Him. And when our old man died, sin was eradicated from our
inmost being. We died to sin.

Jesus didn't just die for us to forgive us. Through our spirit union with
Him, He did something *in* us. He completely solved the sin problem.
He took the sin nature out. As Paul said in Romans 6, he who has died
is freed from—cut off, separated from—sin. Says who? "I do," God says.
"And if you ever catch up with Me, you'll see it."

But if I have died to sin, why am I still tempted to sin? Why do I have this pull within me toward sin? Paul explained that in Romans 7:23. Though sin has been removed from our deepest inner being, it hasn't been eradicated from our body, our "members," as Paul put it. So we can still be pulled by the power of sin that dwells in our body but not in our spirit.

That's why it's so crucial to understand that our old man was crucified with Christ and that we died to sin. We are free from sin. That is a spirit-level truth. Because if we live by our soul's thoughts and feelings, we feel sin's temptation and think that's the real us. It feels as if the real us wants to sin, so we conclude there must still be something wrong with the real us.

To put it in theological terms, it feels like we have both an old nature (our old man) and a new nature (our new creation in Christ). Every outward appearance seems to verify that. The only thing that doesn't is what God says is true: "Knowing this, that our old [man] was crucified with Him…that we would no longer be slaves to sin; for he who has died is freed from sin."

The blood side of the cross labels us FORGIVEN. The body side of the cross labels us THE RIGHTEOUSNESS OF GOD (2 Corinthians 5:21). You're the righteousness of God. You're not just forgiven but perfect and complete. In the unseen and eternal, you are a finished product.

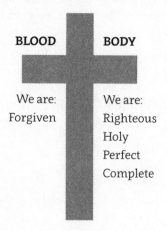

BLOOD   **BODY**

We are: We are:
Forgiven   Righteous
                 Holy
                 Perfect
                 Complete

The old man manifested his nature through us: sins. The new creation in Christ—the new spirit man, born by God's Spirit in righteousness and holiness (Ephesians 4:24)—manifests Christ's nature through us: righteousness. As we learn to live from the truth of what has happened in our spirit, we will witness externally what God has already made an internal reality. We have been separated through death from the power of sin. We have become the righteousness of God. We have a total victory over sin.

So the first thing we died to when we were crucified with Christ is sin. The second thing we died to is the law. The church drowns in confusion over the issue of the law. It has misunderstood it since the first century. Paul's epistle to the Galatians was written to set the record straight on this issue. But much of the church remains confused.

The Scriptures could not be clearer about this. In exactly the same way that Paul said in Romans 6 that we died to sin, in Romans 7 he said that we died to the law:

> Therefore, my brethren, you also were made to die to the Law through the body of Christ, so that you might be joined to another, to Him who was raised from the dead, in order that we might bear fruit for God...But now we have been released from the Law, having died to that by which we were bound, so that we serve in newness of the Spirit and not in oldness of the letter (Romans 7:4,6).

It's not just the ceremonial or civil aspects of the Old Testament law that we have died to. Many teach that. But after Paul stated that we have died to the law, he immediately provided an example—straight from the Ten Commandments: "You shall not covet" (Romans 7:7).

Just as we no longer have any relationship to sin, we no longer have any relationship to the law, including the moral law. Just as sin no longer has any power over us, the law no longer has any power over us. We have died to sin. We have died to the law.

Why did God crucify us to the law? Because although the law is holy and righteous and good (Romans 7:12), it has fulfilled its function in our lives. The law was given that it might reveal sin (Romans 3:20) and lead us to Christ:

> Therefore the Law has become our tutor to lead us to Christ,
> so that we may be justified by faith. But now that faith has
> come, we are no longer under a tutor (Galatians 3:24-25).

Once a person becomes a believer, the law actually hinders the fulfillment of God's purpose for our lives: that He might express His life in and through us. That's because the law by its nature sets a standard that we automatically try in our own effort to live up to. And the moment we do, we are living according to the flesh, from our own self-effort, rather than by faith, trusting Christ's life in us. That is exactly what Paul chastised the Galatians about:

> You foolish Galatians!…did you receive the Spirit by the
> works of the Law, or by hearing with faith? Are you so fool-
> ish? Having begun by the Spirit, are you now being perfected
> by the flesh? (Galatians 3:1-3).

God had to crucify us to the law, because as long as we were married to it (Romans 7:1-3) we were obligated to try (and fail) to keep it on our own. Having been crucified to it, we are free to allow Christ in us to naturally express His life through us. It is not us trying. It is us resting in Him as He produces His righteous fruit. (We will look at the issue of law and grace in more detail in chapter 13.)

The third thing we died to on the cross is ourselves as our point of reference. Paul testified in Galatians 2:20:

> I have been crucified with Christ; and it is no longer I who
> live, but Christ lives in me; and the life which I now live in
> the flesh I live by faith in the Son of God, who loved me and
> gave Himself up for me.

It's impossible for a person to know their union with Christ, and live out of that union, if they don't know they have died with Christ. If I think the old me is still alive, I am still my point of reference. If I am still my point of reference, I am still trying to correct me, straighten me up, make something out of me, or do something to change me. As long as my emphasis is on me, it can't be upon Christ in me. So I'm a divided person. Oh, I can still live in the Romans 7 trap—what I want to do

I don't do; what I don't want to do I do—but I've had enough of that, haven't you? I want to be out of that. What Paul tells us in Romans 6 and 2 Corinthians 5 is that we really *are* out of that.

When Paul poses the question, "Shall we continue in sin just to prove the reality of grace?" he concludes, "People who go on living like that don't really know they died in Christ." In other words, their point of reference hasn't been changed. Their point of reference is still themselves, and they think they're no good and want to sin. Consequently, they're excited about all of this grace of God they can keep drawing on. Paul would say, "Yes, you can keep on drawing on the grace of God for everything you ever do, for every sin you ever commit. But *why*? Why not instead draw on the *life* of God?"

A friend of mine once said to me, "You know, until I really knew that I had been crucified with Christ, there was no way for me to get rid of me. Because I was still alive to me." It's so true. Until we know we've died, we're never going to be free of ourselves, and we will never experience union. We will still be a problem to ourselves. The spotlight will still be on us. That's where most Christians are living their life: "I've got to produce for God."

Until the full work of the cross—our death and resurrection with Christ—becomes a reality to us, we will try to produce something that's not required of us. Our focus will still be on us instead of Christ in us. And we will neglect to be involved in the glorious activity of God as He lives out through us for others. We participate in God's life when we see that we died to ourselves as our point of reference. Christ in us is now our point of reference in all things.

Everything necessary for living the Christian life is provided in the cross, completely and properly understood. It's all in the cross. God hasn't omitted one thing from the cross that is necessary for us to allow Him to live His life through us.

We must experientially know both sides of the cross: Christ died for us (the blood) and we died and were raised with Him (the body).

In the next chapter, we'll look at the "raised with Him" part. For now, it's fundamental to know that you died with Christ. You can't know your union until God has shown you that the old you died. When you died, you died to sin. You died to the law. You died to yourself as your point of reference. As far as being an impediment to God, you are out of the way. The old you is no longer a factor.

It's a great victory to move into the reality of who you are in Christ. You have the privilege of seeing yourself the way God sees you. Your entire point of reference is now Christ who lives in you. You and He are one. He lives His life through you.

We can continue to say, "That can't really mean me, because I know me. I know I'm not dead." Then we'll never know union. We'll never know Christ as our life. We may understand the concept of our death, but not truly know the truth of it in our inner being.

If your death with Christ hasn't become an experiential reality to you yet, I encourage you to ask the Father to make it a reality: "Lord, I want to know. I want to know and experience the truth that I died with Christ. Reveal that to me and make it real in my life."

He will.

5

Doublecross, Part Two: Christ Lives in You

I was riding through Vermont one day, alternately admiring the leaves and reading the New Testament. The Lord directed me to 1 John 4:15, which begins, "Whoever confesses that Jesus is the Son of God..." There is a comma, then the verse continues: "God abides in him, and he in God." I said, "Well, look at that. I confessed Jesus Christ in my early twenties. But I didn't experience the second half of that verse until my midforties. I sat on that comma for almost 25 years!"

Just like the old iron bed, I had sagged in the middle for a very long time. Some days I'd be up, and some days I'd be down. I loved God; I despised God. I wanted to serve Him; I didn't want to serve Him. I got out of bed; I hid in bed. Like most Christians, I was riding a roller coaster: up and down, up and down. But "whoever confesses that Jesus is the Son of God, God abides in him, and he in God." Jesus said, "I am the life." I said to myself, *All along, the life had been resident in me, and I didn't know it.*

In chapter 3 we saw there are two sides to the cross: the blood side and the body side. On the blood side, Jesus Christ died *for* our sins. Through His death for us we obtain forgiveness. On the body side of the cross, in the unseen and eternal realm, in our spirit, we experienced *with* Christ what He experienced: we died with Him and we were raised with Him.

In chapters 3 and 4 we focused on the death aspect of the body side. We died on the cross with Christ. Our old man is dead and buried. We are dead to sin. We are dead to the law. We are dead to ourselves as our point of reference. That we died is foundational truth in the Christian life.

If we emphasize only our death with Christ, however, we will never see what God purposed to be resurrected out of our death: new life. We can stand at the tomb all day celebrating our death and never get on to life. In Romans 6, Paul emphasized both our crucifixion with Christ *and* our resurrection with Him:

> Therefore we have been buried with Him through baptism into death, so that as Christ was raised from the dead through the glory of the Father, so we too might walk in newness of life. For if we have become united with Him in the likeness of His death, certainly we shall be also in the likeness of His resurrection…
>
> Even so consider yourselves to be dead to sin, but alive to God in Christ Jesus (Romans 6:4-5,11).

God raised our new man from the dead and birthed in us an entirely new spirit, holy and righteous, so that He could unite Himself to our spirit and live His life through us. Whether we knew it or not, at salvation Jesus Christ came into us and we became one with Him. He now lives in and through us.

BLOOD   BODY

Christ   Christ
Died   Lives
for   *in*
Us   Us

As with so many New Testament truths, this one is foreshadowed in the Old Testament. In fact, God painted a billboard-sized picture of it. We call it the Passover. In Exodus 12, before God sent the death angel to kill all the firstborn in Egypt, He told the Hebrews to set apart a lamb from the flock, kill it, and smear the blood on the doorposts of their dwellings. When the death angel saw the blood, he would "pass over" that house and spare the firstborn inside. The people only had to apply the blood to the doorposts.

This part of the Passover foretells the blood side of the cross. The lamb died *for* the household. The household didn't participate in that death; the lamb died for them. When they applied its blood to their doorposts, they escaped the wrath of God that came upon the land. Their firstborn son was spared.

The parallel to the blood side of the cross is obvious. Christ died *for* us. He shed His blood as payment for our sins—a satisfaction of the righteous judgment of God. When, by faith, we apply Christ's blood (His death) to our lives, we are spared the wrath of God upon us. Our sins are forgiven.

One day, though, I saw something in the Passover story. When the children of Israel were in captivity under Pharaoh, what country were they in? Egypt. After they put the blood on the doorposts of their houses, and the death angel passed over, and their firstborn son was spared, what country were they still in? Still Egypt.

I saw that as long as our revelation knowledge is limited to the blood side of the cross (Christ dying for us), we may still have our firstborn— that is, our sins are forgiven—but experientially we continue living in captivity. We are still living as if we are subject to the capriciousness of the Pharaohs in our life, in bondage. We are still carnal Christians, striving to overcome by our own effort, trying to become spiritual. It's great to have our sins forgiven. But after a while, living as if we are still captives takes the glamour off being forgiven.

God had a solution to the problem of the Hebrews' captivity. The solution was to provide them with sustenance, or life, to get them out of Egypt. So He instructed each household, after they had smeared the blood of the lamb on the doorposts, to roast the lamb and eat it as nourishment for the upcoming journey. That's the body side of the cross. You take the lamb (Christ) *into* you as life. God is showing us here that the lamb they used for blood on the doorpost was the same lamb they ate for the journey. In other words, everything necessary for living the life comes from the lamb. It isn't that the lamb dies for you and then you're sent out to do the rest on your own (with God's help, of course). The lamb is the total answer. The lamb that gave its blood for them also gave its life to them. They took its meat into them, and that became their nourishment, strength, and vitality for the journey. They lived their life out of the lamb's life. They walked in its energy. They killed one lamb for two purposes: for the Passover and for the walk.

Paul calls the New Testament life a walk. What is the sustenance, the life, of that walk? It isn't us trying to walk for God. It may look like that on the outside, but we have taken the Lamb of God into us. He is not only the forgiveness of our sins. He is also the life within us, from whom we make the journey.

One cross fulfills both purposes, just as there was one lamb for two purposes. God says, "Take the blood and put it on your door. Take the meat and put it in your body. Put the life in you. Unless you put the life in you, you'll always be operating in the realm of captivity. When you put the life in you, you'll be ready to live. You'll be ready to start the journey."

We can walk around for years with a sense of forgiveness but no sense of life. We have the life in us, but we don't know it. We try to generate the life ourselves, but we are doomed to failure because it's impossible for us to generate the life. God is telling us, "I will share My glory with no man. Only I can live My life. But I will impart the life to you. I will give you the life. I will live it through you."

That's why there isn't anything beyond the grace of God, completely understood, that is necessary for living the Christian life. All you're ever going to need for life is in the cross—both sides of the cross. It's all in Christ. And He is in us. Paul wrote:

> For if while we were enemies we were reconciled to God through the death of His Son, much more, having been reconciled, we shall be saved by His life (Romans 5:10).

We are saved not just by Christ's death, but also by Christ's life. That's true eternally, but it's also true in the here and now. We are saved by the life of Christ that lives within us.

In John 6, Jesus feeds the five thousand from five loaves and two fish. He leaves, but the crowd tracks him down, wanting more. He tells them, in essence, "You didn't see the miracle in the miracle. You saw the seen and temporal multiplication of bread. But you didn't see the unseen and eternal miracle. I am the unseen and eternal miracle." Jesus isn't just a bread-producer. He's a life-giver. Later in John 6, He says, "I am the bread of life…Unless you eat the flesh of the Son of Man and drink His blood, you have no life in yourselves. He who eats My flesh and drinks My blood has eternal life." We have eternal life in us—God's life. It's the life without beginning and without end. It's the uncreated life.

Jesus is telling us, "I am all a person needs for living the life. It isn't Me plus something. It isn't Me plus your prayer life. It isn't Me plus your Bible study. It isn't Me plus your good service. It isn't Me plus the sum of everything you can do, because you will never produce a life that pleases Me. I am the only life that pleases Me."

Nobody is offended as long as you are talking from the perspective of separation instead of union. As long as we are down here and God is up there, and He does something *for* us, it's okay. But when you start talking about Jesus living His life *in* you, *through* you, *as* you, that raises eyebrows. In John 6, the people were perfectly satisfied with Jesus as long as He produced bread. The offense came when He said He *was* the bread. "How can this man give us His flesh to eat?" they asked.

Jesus was telling the Jews, "You're doing all these external things, but there isn't any life in that." The opposite of life is death. If we're not operating out of the life, we're operating out of death. But it doesn't look like death because often we get results. Church programs get results. Our personal programs get results. On the seen and temporal level we *are* getting results. Jesus has a word for people about that: "There's your reward. You're getting *your* results. So there's your reward. Go ahead with it. But it isn't of Me. It is not My life flowing through you."

Paul revealed the secret of the life of Christ in us. To the Galatians he said, "I live, but no, I don't. Christ lives in me. It looks like me, but it's

Christ." To the Colossians he wrote, "It's Christ in you that's your hope of glory." To the Philippians he proclaimed: "For me, to live is Christ." Who was doing the living? Christ. But if you looked right at him, who would it look like? Paul.

Paul illustrated this in 2 Corinthians 5:20: "We are ambassadors for Christ, as though God were making an appeal through us." These ambassadors for Christ were pleading with the Gentiles. But who was really pleading? God was making His plea through them. The words and the works came through Paul. But Paul knew he wasn't working up this concern for Gentiles. God was in him making that appeal. It looked like Paul, but it was the indwelling Jesus.

What does the life of God living through us look like? For our primary example we have to go no further than the Gospels. Jesus said,

> "Come to Me, all who are weary and heavy-laden, and I will
> give you rest. Take My yoke upon you and learn from Me...
> and you will find rest for your souls. For My yoke is easy and
> My burden is light" (Matthew 11:28-30).

I often wondered, *What did He mean, "Learn from Me?"* As I looked through the Gospel of John, I found the answer. I saw Jesus making statements over and over like:

> "I don't do anything of myself."

> "I only do what I see with the Father."

> "I only speak what I hear from the Father."

> "The works that I do, they're not My works, they're the Father's
> works who dwells in Me."

When Jesus said, "Learn from Me," He meant to learn from Him how He lived. And how did He live? He lived out of the Father. He didn't have any other secret. As author Gene Edwards has said, Jesus Christ never tried to live the Christian life. He didn't have a Bible at home to read; He didn't have a prayer group to go to. He let the Father live the life through Him. He learned how to live out of the resources of the Father, which are not of this seen and temporal realm, but of the unseen and eternal realm.

Jesus could have phrased it, "The Father is my life." All of His state-ments above witness to that. The Father was living His life through Jesus. We could summarize Jesus's statements like this: "What you see when you look at Me is the Father as Me." He and the Father were one. The Father lived through Him as Him. Jesus was at rest in that. The Jews were infuriated by that, because it seemed blasphemous.

The life of the Son was the Father, and the life of the sons is the Son. So how do you live the life? You learn to live out of the Son and the Father. To learn to live out of the Son and the Father, though, you have to know where the Son and the Father live—in you. It's a miracle. It's amaz-ing. It can't be fully explained. But it can be witnessed in the life of Christ.

After my sins were forgiven, my question was always, "How do you live the life?" What I discovered was this: you don't. Because you can't.

For years I regarded myself as my point of origin. But I couldn't pro-duce the life of God out of me. I couldn't bring the uncreated (God's life) out of the creation (me). How was I going to do that? As long as I saw myself as the source of life, though, I had to keep trying. Until one day Jesus impressed this upon my spirit: "I am your life. I am the only life acceptable to the Father. I not only want to forgive you; I want to live the life in you. I want to be your life."

I was looking back through Romans 6 one day. My focus typically jumped from verse 7 ("He who has died is freed from sin.") to verse 11 ("Consider yourselves to be dead to sin but alive to God in Christ Jesus."). But that day my attention was drawn to verse 10: "For the death that [Jesus] died, He died to sin, once for all; but the life that He lives, He lives to God."

The life that Jesus lives, *He lives to God*. And where is Jesus? He is in us. Jesus in us naturally lives His life unto God. He *only* lives unto God. We don't have to *try* to live for God. We don't have to *try* to live the life. He in us lives it. If we know that the old us is dead and out of the way, we can rest assured that the Person in us is going to live for the glory of God. Jesus said, "My food is to do the will of Him who sent Me and to accomplish His work" (John 4:34). That's who lives in us. His only desire and will is to do the will of the Father. He lives in you and me, and He will do it.

When you boil it all down, we only have three big questions: Who is the life? Where is the life? Who am I? When we get those settled, life is easy.

Jesus is the life. He lives in me. I am a vessel, a container of His life, holy and righteous and blameless in His sight. If I know who the life is and where the life is, I am free from trying to become something I was never meant to be. It's easy to be natural. It's hard to be unnatural. When you're trying to be unnatural—trying to produce the life on your own—what results? Frustration, anger, desperation. Finally you want to give up. I know I did.

We're not meant to operate unnaturally. But if I know who I am, and who the life is, and where the life is, I can just be myself and let Him live it. Because no one has trouble being themselves.

You may be on the verge of an "Oh, I see," concerning this. "I see how to live the life. I let Him live it." If so, I want to encourage you to reckon yourself dead. The old you is dead. Count on it. Reckon yourself alive to God in Christ Jesus. He is the One in you that lives to God. Count on Him to be doing it, moment by moment. By faith reckon yourself dead as your point of reference. Stop looking at yourself and your performance. You are holy and blameless in His sight. Christ in you is your point of reference. He is always sufficient, always loving, always living unto the Father.

It's not your striving that releases Christ's life through you. It's your trusting. Just say, "Lord, Your Holy Spirit is showing me this truth. I embrace it by faith, just like I embraced Jesus *for* me by faith and experienced forgiveness of my sins. I now embrace Jesus *in* me as my life. Teach me, convince me of this truth by the Holy Spirit, so that I won't be captive any longer to trying to produce the life myself."

What's good news to us now isn't just that He died *for* us, though that is good news. It isn't just that He's *with* us, though that is good news. It isn't just that He's *in* us, *helping* us, though that is good news. The really good news is that He is in us, *living His life as us*. He has joined His Spirit with our spirit. In the unseen and eternal, there's Deity inside us. We are not that Deity, but we are containers of that Deity.

A well of eternal life is springing up within us. That life is adequate; that life is sufficient; that life is never exhausted, never tires, never tastes bitter. That life is always light, always has mercy in it, always has a second chance in it, always carries God's forgiveness toward others, always is love.

When we recognize this, suddenly the *oughts* and the *musts* of Satan's frenetic life become the "Be still, and be" of God's life—the "Be still, and be" of His eternal presence. A dramatic change of our point of reference results. Satan's invitation to humanity was "you become." When we're playing the game of *must* and *ought*, we're in the spotlight. Our performance is center stage. But our point of reference is now the indwelling Jesus Christ. He has no part in the separation implied by *must* and *ought*. He lives in our inner sanctuary, the Holy of Holies, where all simply *is*. We are invited to let that be, and let Him come forth.

6

One Spirit

People love mysteries. At the movies, on television, and in bestselling books, mysteries abound: murder mysteries, spy mysteries, crime mysteries, political intrigue—the list seems endless. Life, too, presents us with many mysteries. "Why am I here? What does my life mean? Where am I going?"

Some truths lie so far beyond our intellectual grasp that we can't understand them, yet we can't deny them either. These too are mysteries.

Mysteries defy this world's interpretations. Without revelation, we will never understand a mystery. Common sense or man's intellect will never understand a mystery in the spiritual realm. We can probe it, study it, analyze it, define it, but doing those things doesn't mean we have understood or experienced that mystery.

Jesus used parables to explain mystery. He would tell the disciples, "It has been given to you to know the mysteries of the kingdom of heaven." They would say, "It has? Well, that's news to us!" He would tell a parable and they would reply, "Tell us what it means!"

Jesus's teaching often seemed like a mystery even apart from parables. In John 14, Jesus told the disciples, "If you've seen Me, you've seen the Father."

Philip responded, "Show us the Father, and we will be satisfied."

Jesus answered, "Have I been so long with you, and you haven't come to know Me, Philip? He who has seen Me has seen the Father. How do you say, 'Show us the Father'?"

The New Testament writers constantly employed below-the-line illustrations to explain above-the-line realities. John, in particular, used everyday experiences in his Gospel to illustrate the spirit realm. In chapter 3, he told how Jesus used physical birth to illustrate spiritual birth. In chapter 4, he wrote of Jesus comparing physical places of worship with the true place of worship, the spirit. In chapter 6, he paralleled the physical bread Jesus multiplied to Jesus Himself as the Bread of Life. Repeatedly he wrote about things people could understand to explain things that were still beyond them.

Paul's teaching to believers focused on a great mystery. To the church in Colossae he wrote of

> the *mystery* which has been hidden from the past ages and generations, but has now been manifested to His saints, to whom God willed to make known what is the riches of the glory of this *mystery* among the Gentiles, which is *Christ in you*, the hope of glory (Colossians 1:26-27).

Christ *in* us. That is our only expectation of experiencing and expressing the glory of God. Elsewhere, Paul expressed the mystery in another way:

> But he who is joined to the Lord is one spirit with Him (1 Corinthians 6:17, NKJV).

Actually, the words *with Him* aren't even in the original Greek. The translators added them for clarification. So:

> He who is joined to the Lord is one spirit.

He or she, a spiritual being, who is joined to the Lord, is one spirit. There are two…yet they are one. You and He are one.

We are one spirit with God. We function as one. We are not absorbed into the Lord, however. There is an "I" and there is a "He," but we are joined to Him and we function as one. It is a function of cooperation, like a union of gears that mesh together. Our union with God doesn't mean we're so swallowed up in God that we lose our identity. But neither is there a separation. Rather, the two function as one for the purposes of the greater one, God.

He that is joined to the Lord is one spirit. That is a mystery. One plus one equals one. How can that be? The divine and the human are one.

Until we know and live out of our union with Christ, we will never fully manifest the life of God within us. Some of it will inevitably shine through now and then, despite us. But for the most part we will manifest our own merely human life.

Until we know union, we are constantly confronted by the illusion of separation. "God is up there; I am down here. How do I draw close to God? Give me a plan. Give me a program." Plenty of people are ready with the answers. "Read your Bible. Pray. Study. Witness. Tithe. Take communion. Here are the plans. Here are the programs."

But once you know your union with God, there's nothing left for you to do. Oh, you may still do some of the outer things. But you aren't doing them to get close to God. You and God are one. There is no more separation.

When you begin living out of your union with Jesus Christ, you move beyond Christ plus anything, no matter how good it might be. You're out on the thinnest limb on the branch. There isn't anything else for you to turn to. You have left behind all the old clothes of "You ought to do this" and "You ought to do that" and "If you do this, there will be these kinds of results." That stuff will work, on a certain level, to a certain point. But you're not there anymore. You've moved into the realm of He and you are one. You have entered His rest.

God is a Spirit Being in union with your spirit being. You are in God. He is in you. He lives as you. All the life comes through you. But you know that it isn't you. You know it's really Christ in you *as* you. You have a full, complete, perfect union.

If we know we are in union with Christ, we won't live as if in separation anymore. We may visit there occasionally, but that won't be home to us. We won't live in self-consciousness anymore. We live and move and have our being in God, who is our life. We are saved by His life. He *is* our life. We don't try to draw life from the Tree of the Knowledge of Good and Evil, and all of its dos and don'ts. We learn to be at home in the Tree of Life. The Tree of Life is not a way, a principle, a doctrine, nor a law. It is a Person: Jesus Christ.

Christ lives out His life in us—funny old you, funny old me. We have all kinds of different shapes, forms, and fashions, all kinds of interests, all kinds of diversity, all kinds of uniqueness. Praise the Lord. We don't have to look like, act like, talk like, or be like anybody else again. We are free to be ourselves. People see us, but we know it's Jesus living through us.

God spoke to me concerning my union with Him during my most difficult physical trial to date. In 1994 I was diagnosed with stage-four colon cancer. I said, "What's going on, Lord? What's this all about?"

He began to minister to me. I sensed His voice saying, "Nothing's changed. I already knew you had cancer. The only thing that has changed is you found out what I knew." According to my son-in-law, a doctor, I had probably had cancer quite awhile because it had metastasized from my colon to my liver.

But God had more things to say to me. He said, "Nothing has changed, because I've always loved you. I'm loving you now. And I will continue to love you."

And He said this: "You're going to get everything done that I want you to get done." That's what I heard in my spirit.

I spent a couple of days in the hospital convalescing, thinking about these things, and seeking the Lord about them. After a while it's as if the question arose within me from Him: "Now, where are you going to live? Are you going to live in 'my body has cancer'? Or are you going to live in the Spirit?"

"I'm going to live in the Spirit," I replied. And God showed me again what it meant to be in union with Him.

He said to me, impressing upon my spirit, "Who are you in union with?"

"I'm in union with You," I answered.

"Well, who am I?"

"You are the uncreated One. You are before time, and You are after time is over."

That's the internal conversation I was having with the Lord. When you and He talk like that, you know to whom you're talking and from whom you're hearing.

"That's right. That's who I am. And you are joined to Me, aren't you?"

"Yes."

"So that means you don't have an end, either. You're a part of My family."

I said to myself, *That's who I am in union with. And cancer can't touch that. Cancer can't touch the real me, or Him in me. Outside, I may have cancer. But inside I have the Living God, with whom I am one.*

As with so many above-the-line truths, the mystery of our union with God has its parallel below the line. It's first mentioned at the very beginning, in Genesis 2:24:

> For this reason a man shall leave his father and his mother, and
> be joined to his wife; and they shall become one flesh.

The two shall become one flesh. Genesis 4:1-2 says that Adam knew his wife and the firstborn came; Adam knew his wife again and the second born came. God gave to the first two, to humankind, male and female, the right to reproduce and bring forth humankind. Except for the unique way that Jesus our Lord was conceived (and ignoring our modern reproductive technologies), we've done it that way ever since. Everybody got here by the natural process.

I'm using a below-the-line illustration we are very familiar with. But as I do, think in terms of spirit. Think above the line. He that is joined to the Lord is one spirit.

God has given to humankind, male and female, the task, the joy, the privilege of reproducing their own selves. Each mate brings his or her function. That's very important. One implants. The other manifests.

There hasn't been a male yet who manifested a child. There hasn't been a female yet who implanted a child. But as one—*as one*—with each performing their God-given function, we reproduce ourselves. He that is joined to the she is one flesh. Out of that physical union comes the life of the seed. The male implants the seed; the female bears the child.

He that is joined to the she is one flesh. He that is joined to the Lord is one spirit. Of course, in this modern age we know a lot more about what happens during reproduction than they did in the Bible era. We know that both mother and father contribute equally to the genetic makeup of the child. But what I'm doing is drawing the illustration as the people understood it back then. They knew the male implanted the seed; they knew the female bore the child.

Now, let's go above the line. If he that is joined to the Lord is one spirit, who provides the seed? Who provides the life? God the Spirit. Who manifests the offspring? We do.

Men, this is difficult for us to realize, but whether we are a pro football player or a rodeo bull rider or an accountant or a preacher, there's no place for macho male thinking here. Above the line, we are female. We are expressers. Manifestors. We don't originate anything in the realm of the spirit. Humankind, both male and female, simply expresses the life. God's Spirit produces the life of the seed. We don't produce a thing. We manifest the seed.

What we produce on our own is filthy rags. We produce our own work, our own effort. What you and I reproduce if we try is our flesh. And there's no life in the flesh.

What Paul wrote in 1 Corinthians 6:17 ("He who is joined to the Lord is one spirit with Him"), he gave autobiographical expression to in Galatians 2:20: "I have been crucified with Christ; and it is no longer I who live, but Christ lives in me."

What does he mean? It is no longer *I* living as my point of reference in life. It is no longer *I* living as my point of origin for life. Jesus Christ is the only origin of life in me.

Remember, in the spiritual realm, all of us are females. In the physical realm, if a woman wants to have a child, no amount of "I want to," no amount of thinking, no amount of trying on her own, will produce a child. To illustrate this, I used to play a game with the gals and say, "Let's sit here and decide we want to be pregnant. Let's say it for nine months: 'I'm pregnant. I'm pregnant. I'm pregnant. I'm pregnant.' After nine months what are you going to bear? Nothing. *Nothing!*"

That illustrates a spiritual truth. The flesh profits nothing. The flesh produces nothing. For someone to stand in the pulpit Sunday after Sunday and tell you what you *ought* to do is a curse on you, because you can't produce it. Have you tried? I did, until the Holy Spirit showed me this:

You are dead as a point of origin. Christ in you is the point of origin. He will live the life in you as you.

That's how Jesus lived. He would say, in essence, "I don't do anything except what the Father does." The Father lived His life in Jesus, and it looked like Jesus, didn't it? The people always went to see Jesus. They always went to hear Jesus. They always went to Jesus to heal them. But Jesus didn't do anything—except manifest. He manifested the life of the Father who was in Him.

I'm no authority on this question, but I have been around it three times: Ladies, when you get pregnant, can you keep from manifesting it? We couldn't at my house. You can't, either. That illustrates a spiritual truth.

You went through those months with the first one, and you felt the first movement of life, and you asked your husband to put his hand on your tummy, and both of you felt life. You hadn't seen it yet. But you felt it. You experienced it. And in the fullness of time, you brought forth your firstborn, and your second born, and your third born. Because you had the seed.

It's a mystery. Christ in you, the hope of glory. You have received the life. You cannot—*you cannot*—fail to manifest it. We have spent our life concentrating on when we foul up. God spends His time on our side, seeing when we do express Him.

The mystery, hidden from the past ages and generations but revealed to us, is this: Christ in you. Not your life but His. Not you producing His life, but you expressing His life, as you by faith trust Him to live through you, as you.

Part Two

Soul and Spirit

7

The Swing

About 20 years into my Christian life, I reached a point of crisis. I mentioned it in chapter 1. I was a God-lover, but I discovered that given the right set of circumstances I was capable of doing anything I might have done when I was lost. Something happened in my affections temporarily and I saw what I was capable of. I did nothing for which I am ashamed, but God allowed Satan to reveal a latent potential in me, causing me to despise myself. What I found out later was this: I got into that mess by not knowing the difference between soul and spirit.

At the time, I was part of a group that was very feeling oriented. I wanted good feelings, and I got them. I stayed on a high for six months. My mildly manic-depressive temperament made me think, *Boy, I'm out of this up-and-down life now. I've got this sucker on a smooth plain. I'm up here in the stratosphere and all is wonderful. I'm really sailing. Good feelings and good vibes all over the place.*

Then I started having this affection, this feeling, for another woman. And it got my attention. Here I was having a feeling that, if carried out, would have been the most foolish thing I could ever do—a sin against my marriage and God. I was enjoying the feeling, but I had enough morality to know it was wrong. So I was in a dilemma. I was looking for good feelings, but now I was enjoying a good feeling that was terribly wrong.

That's when I got mad at God and sent Him my letter of resignation.

A short time later, as I mentioned earlier, Barbara asked me to read *Power in Praise*, in which I read that verse: "In everything give thanks; for this is God's will for you in Christ Jesus" (1 Thessalonians 5:18). I began to thank God in spite of my feelings, and before long I got some insight. At the level of my feelings, I was mad at God. But in the spirit realm—which I wasn't paying any attention to and didn't really know—I heard that verse I read, and it was life to me.

So I discovered that within me I could be two places at the same time: on the one hand, angry with God, and on the other, some part of me hearing and responding to God despite my anger. I wanted to know the difference between these two things happening in me simultaneously because I saw what living out of my feelings could do to me.

Someone pointed me to Hebrews 4, starting with verse 9:

> So there remains a Sabbath rest for the people of God. For the one who has entered His rest *has himself also rested from his works*, as God did from His. Therefore let us be diligent to enter that rest, so that no one will fall, through following the same [Israelite] example of disobedience (4:9-11).

That's where I had been: in my works. I was still doing the self thing, "doing good for God." I had thought, *I've finally got this thing going. You do this, this, and this, and God is always blessing you. He gives you these nice, cozy feelings.*

But I didn't know union with Christ. If you enter God's rest you cease from your own works, as God did from His. I wanted to enter His rest. I continued to read:

> For the word of God is living and active and sharper than any two-edged sword, and piercing as far as the division of soul and spirit...

The Holy Spirit didn't speak to me through that clause, because I didn't understand it.

> ...of both joints and marrow...

He didn't speak to me through that phrase. I was no physician; I didn't know the difference between joints and marrow.

...and able to judge [discern] the thoughts and intentions of
the heart (Hebrews 4:12).

Wait a minute now, I said to myself. When the Spirit spoke to me
through that word, my spirit caught it. I said, *Oh, I see. The thoughts and
intentions of the heart are two different things. I see that in one area of you—
your thoughts and emotions—you can be experiencing one thing, and in
another—in the spirit realm—you can be at another place.*

That had happened to me two times in a row. In the first, my affections were going one direction, but within me I knew that was wrong.
Later, my soul was pouting at God, but in my spirit I was hearing Him
and responding to Him.

So there was a difference between the thoughts and intentions of
my heart. As a believer, I knew the intent of my heart. It was fixed. The
intent of my heart was for God. Even when my life was on that up-and-
down roller coaster, the intent of my heart was for God. But I could have
thoughts and feelings that differed from the intent of my heart. For the
first time in my awareness, I was experiencing the reality of spirit. I was
conscious of it in a way that made a difference in my life.

Listening to people for years, talking to them about their problems
and their ups and downs, I have concluded this: very few Christians
know the difference between soul and spirit. We confuse our feelings
and thoughts with our real self, our deepest inner person, our spirit. The
problem is that our thoughts and feelings are so much louder to most of
us than the intent of our heart. We haven't experienced the living Word
of God to separate soul from spirit. The living Word of God that the
Spirit speaks into our heart is sharp, like a sword, and it divides, making
a sharp distinction between soul and spirit.

We're not just feelings and thoughts, or soul. We're spirit beings. God
is the Father of our spirit (John 3:6 and Hebrews 12:9). Our spirit is one
with Him (1 Corinthians 6:17). Our spirit lives in union with Him. But
that union of spirit is so quiet. It's noiseless. It doesn't cause the same
uproar within us that thoughts and feelings do. If we don't know the
nature of spirit, the rumblings of our soul can confuse us. Then we begin
to think, *That's the real me. Those thoughts and feelings are the real me.*

That's how we start believing we have two natures. We have thoughts
or feelings we don't like, and we conclude that part of the real us must

still be bad. I have those kinds of thoughts and feelings off and on all day long. Don't you? Our thoughts and feelings can run the gamut on any given day. So we start battling the ones we don't like, trying to bring them under submission. And the harder we try to exert power over them, the more tightly they seem to grab us.

To experience our union with Christ, the Holy Spirit has to give us revelation on two truths. First, we have to have a revelation that we died in Christ, that we are dead to sin, dead to the law, and dead to ourselves as our point of reference.

Second, we have to have a revelation on the difference between soul and spirit and how to manage it. Until these two truths become fixed in our spiritual consciousness, we're never truly going to live out of union. Satan will keep telling us, "The old you isn't really dead. These thoughts and feelings are the real you. Aren't you ashamed to be such a wretched sinner as to have such thoughts and feelings?"

Years ago I was pastoring a church in Saint Petersburg, Florida. Being from Kentucky, my family had never been in a hurricane, but a hurricane was heading our way. So we turned on the radio for the latest update. The weatherman was saying, "The wind will be ferocious, so seek a place of security and safety. But when a period of dead silence comes, don't leave your place of safety. Because after that period of silence, you will be hit by the back side of the hurricane." If during the silence someone said, "It's all over," and came charging out, the next place they might have landed was in Ohio. So that was good advice: don't leave your place of security.

The hurricane illustrates the difference between spirit and soul. The eye of the hurricane is dead quiet, yet people who understand hurricanes know that the life and power of the hurricane is in that eye. But where is all the noise and fuss? It's out in the soul. The spirit is fixed, unified, quiet. The soul is turbulent. It's making all kinds of noise and spewing forth all kinds of emotions, and we ride the crest of its waves. That's the way we experience life. On the soul level we have our up-and-down feelings and our up-and-down thoughts. That's where all the activity is taking place. And if we don't know who we really are—spirit persons—and that our spirit is in union with God, then the soul activity will control us.

Often you will see the various parts of our makeup illustrated this way:

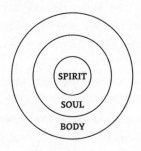

All three parts constitute the whole us. We are spirit, soul, *and* body. But which is the most important of the three? Spirit. Our spirit is the part of us that is born from above (John 3). It is, we could say, the true us, our deepest identity. The soul is changeable. The spirit is fixed.

We can illustrate the operation of spirit and soul by a swing or pendulum. The top of the swing, where the rope is attached, is our spirit. That's where the swing is joined to its anchor or place of security. That's where things are safe. It may make a little movement, but compared to the movement of the swing it makes no movement at all. It's the quiet place. You don't pay any attention to it. A child doesn't pay any attention to where a swing is fixed. He or she just jumps in the seat and starts swinging.

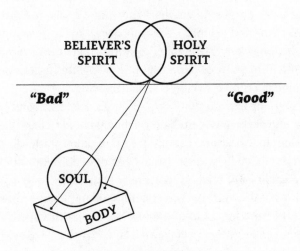

Just as the top of the swing is attached to a secure foundation, our spirit is joined to the ultimate Anchor, the Lord Himself. Our spirit makes little or no noise or movement. It is fixed. It is quiet, safe, and at rest. Our spirit exists in the unseen and eternal realm where things simply *are*. It doesn't change; it isn't variable. Our union with God doesn't fluctuate.

As with the top of the swing, ordinarily we don't pay much attention to our spirit. In an important sense, we can do the same with God, our Anchor. I'm not saying we are complacent toward Him; rather, we can always depend on Him. After all, He's the secure one. He isn't going to let go. He isn't going to turn us loose. We belong to Him. We're His possession, for whom He gladly gave His life.

The bottom of the swing, the swing seat, represents soul and body. These include our thoughts and emotions, plus our five senses and all other physical aspects of our being. Of course, the body exists entirely in the seen and temporal realm. What is easy to overlook is that the soul *operates* in that realm as well. Unlike the realm of spirit, the soul is not unchanging or fixed. It changes every second, as soon as a new thought or feeling comes along. Anything beyond the union of His Spirit and your spirit belongs to the natural order and is external to spirit reality.

What is the purpose of a swing? To swing. Go out and put a little child in a swing and tell him, "You can't swing. You're not supposed to swing." It won't work. He is going to swing. That's the purpose of the thing. And if the purpose of a swing is to swing, it isn't performing its proper function until it swings. It's made to swing.

But we don't like our swing to swing. Our soul fluctuates between thoughts and feelings we don't like and thoughts and feelings we do like, and we don't like those fluctuations. If we don't know spirit, all we know within us is our wildly swinging soul. Most of us don't know God's rest, the full grace of God, and how to live out of our union, so we try to stop that swing because our soul's fluctuations are unpleasant to us and it seems as if God wants us to stop them. We think that Christian maturity is getting that swing under control. So we try to take our swing and nail it up on what we think is God's side.

ETERNAL

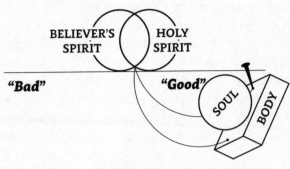

TEMPORAL

But where we try to nail it up isn't really God's side. It's not the place from which the life of Christ flows, because it's not originating above the line, from the union of our spirit with God's Spirit. Rather, it's *good's* side. Now, good might be God, but what I'm calling good isn't always God.

To put it another way, we are operationally still eating from the Tree of the Knowledge of Good and Evil rather than from the Tree of Life, which is Christ. We are trying to eat from the Good side of that Tree, trying to always maintain good thoughts and good feelings and, certainly, good behavior.

Whether we're eating from the Good side or the Evil side, however, we're still eating from the wrong tree. We're still operating out of our own effort, which cannot produce God's life. Our self-effort isn't originating above the line, from the union of our spirit with God's Spirit. It's not flowing from the life of Christ. It's originating below the line, from our soul operating independently and trying to make us "good" Christians.

As long as our point of reference is our soul, then our point of reference is still ourselves, vacillating between thinking and feeling good and thinking and feeling bad. We're trying to stop that swing because we think God wants us to stop all those bad feelings and thoughts. So we try to nail the swing up on the good side.

But we're never going to get the swing stopped because God put it into motion. God designed us on the soul level to be capable of feeling and thinking things that are contrary to spirit reality. Why? *Because that is the only way we can learn to live by faith out of who we really are and who He really is, rather than out of appearances.* God uses the operation of the swing to push us into living out of spirit, where we are joined to Him.

(I'm not saying here that it is irrelevant what we set our mind upon. What we choose to set our mind upon is important, as I will later discuss. I am referring to the endless stream of thoughts and feelings that cross our mind and emotions, the appearing of which we have no control over.)

God put our humanity into motion for His own eternal purposes, making it capable of all kinds of feelings and thoughts. So if we try to stop it, we're doomed to failure. How are we going to stop what God started? But we have the illusion that we can. We call it crucifying the self. Maybe for six weeks we get this whole process under control, and we get this swing nailed up over on good's side, and we say, "Whew! I have learned the secret." About the time we turn our back, however, thinking we've got it made, the swing comes loose and smacks us in the fanny. And we say, "Well, I don't have it after all." So we go back under guilt.

Our point of reference is still ourselves, our soul, rather than Christ in us. We're trying to stop something about which God is saying, "It's okay, it's okay. I made you that way. You aren't supposed to get that swing stopped." We're going to try to stop the swing until we see that it's what God meant to happen. Once we can see that God has put it into operation, then we don't have to feel condemned anymore.

As long as our own humanity is our point of reference, we don't know we died and we can't know union. We *can't* know it. I didn't say we couldn't talk about it or quote Bible verses about it. I'm saying we can't have an experiential knowledge of our union. But when we experience the reality of our union with Christ, we are no longer a soul-based person, a person that sees ourselves as our point of reference. We have moved to another place altogether.

That's when we begin to see our soul activity not as a negative in our life but as a positive. When our soul isn't our point of reference anymore, but rather our spirit joined to God, then our attention is taken off our soul and directed toward Him.

When we see who we really are in Christ, then we can say, "This swing is absolutely necessary in God's scheme of things, because how can the principle of faith operate in me without fluctuations on my soul level? How can faith operate in me if I can't be tempted to have unfaith?"

The deepest level is where you and God are joined together as one. As you begin to live from there, you're no longer validating either God or yourself from your soul. So your soul ceases to be a real problem area for you. As long as you are living below the line, your soul and body are problem areas for you. You validate God when you're well and not sick. You validate God when your soul activity is "good" and not "bad." But when you're living from spirit, you don't have to validate God from your soul or body. You validate God from your spirit.

The Spirit of God, in union with your spirit, doesn't make any noise. What makes noise is your soul: your feelings and your thoughts. I wish I could get them quiet. Don't you? But we can't because we're not meant to. We're meant to live *in the midst* of the noise (about which we will go into further detail in chapters 17 and 18). But we live *from*—we draw our life from—that place of perfect stillness and quietness, where all simply *is*, where we know that we know. When God has revealed to us true spirit union, we make our decisions from Him, and they are based on an inner knowing. No one else may see or understand that knowing, but *we* will know it.

The Spirit of God is never going to make a lot of noise in your life. He says to us, "You'd better know Me or you'll miss Me. Because My starting point is not going to be in your feelings. My starting point is not going to be in your thoughts. That doesn't mean that I won't come through them, but that's not My starting point. My starting point is in your spirit. I am one with your spirit."

Your spirit doesn't know by analysis. It knows by revelation. You know God by revelation. By revelation you know that you and God are one. By revelation you know that He uses the below-the-line activities of your life to express His life by means of you. Once you know that, the fluctuations of your soul are no longer a source of self-condemnation.

What used to be a problem area for you becomes the area of God's activity, to bring you into a life of faith. Then others see the life of God coming through you.

My favorite Bible illustration of soul and spirit is the story of Elijah. Elijah was a mighty man of God. He did something I've never done. He said, "It's not going to rain anymore until I say so." That got folks' attention. And sure enough, it didn't rain for three years. He was a great man of God, but he had a lot of soul noise in his life, good and bad.

Elijah lived in a time of pagan worship and ungodliness in Israel. His conflict with the apostates came to a head when he told King Ahab to assemble all of Israel and the prophets of Baal on Mount Carmel for a showdown, to prove who was truly God (1 Kings 18). In the contest, the prophets' false god couldn't produce fire, but Elijah called down fire from heaven. After God had proven Himself, Elijah killed all 450 false prophets. He was riding high.

Let me give you my paraphrase of the rest of the story.

That night King Ahab went back home to the castle, to his wife, the evil Queen Jezebel. It was the maid's day off, and Jezzie was in the kitchen, tossing a salad. She was up to her elbows in lettuce and carrots and peppers, and she was preparing her special Jezzie's Juice for dressing. Ahab walked in and said, "Jezzie, you should have been at the revival today."

"You know I don't have anything to do with your religion." She kept working on that salad.

"You would have seen something today," he replied. "It was amazing." Then he told her about the contest.

"I'm not interested in your religion, Ahab. I've got my own gods. I've got my own preachers."

He answered, "Well, I want to tell you about that. I believe you are now preacherless. Because after the contest was over, Elijah took all of your preachers, all 450 of them, down by the brook and killed them."

"What did you say?!"

"All of your preachers are dead."

Jezebel started picking the lettuce off her hands, slowly. She instructed Ahab, "Go in my office and get me a piece of royal stationery. Get me the royal pen and the royal ink. I'm going to write a royal letter." Ahab, the henpecked husband, ran and got the royal paper, pen, and ink and brought them to her. Jezebel wrote one sentence: "By this time tomorrow, you're going to be as dead as all of my preachers."

She folded it, sealed it with the royal seal, and said, "Take that out to Elijah. He's sitting out there in the town square with all those other wise guys. Take that to him!"

So Elijah got the letter. And this fearless man of God stood up and said, "I'll face her! I'm not afraid of her! I'll meet her tomorrow and she won't kill me. God is going to triumph."

Is that what he did?

Not exactly.

Elijah declared, "I think it's time for my annual vacation, and I'll take it without pay." He didn't even wait around for the treasurer's check. He lit out. He ran. The Bible says that he was afraid. He feared for his life.

Fear is an emotion. It's in the soul. At that moment, like so many of us, Elijah was motivated by his soul activity. He was living just like any other person, living out of the deepest thing that he understood about himself, his thoughts and feelings. So when Jezebel threatened his life, he made a decision based on those thoughts and feelings. He fled. He made the only response he could make based on the level he was functioning within. We can't fault him for that. If Elijah had been operating at the deepest level of himself, the spirit level, he wouldn't have needed the lesson God was about to give him.

Elijah ran to Mount Horeb and hid in a cave. That's where God encountered him. God said (again, my paraphrase), "What are you doing here, Elijah? I thought I left you up at Carmel rejoicing and leading the congregation in celebration. You were having quite a revival."

Elijah answered, "The queen threatened to kill me and I had to run, because I'm the only one you've got left."

"Are you the only one I have left?" God replied. "Well, poor Me. I want to tell you something, Elijah. I've got 6999 others, and you make 7000."

"Oh."

God said, "Elijah, go stand at the mouth of the cave. I'm going to perform an outdoor drama for you. I'm going to pass by you." Then God passed before Elijah in the form of an earthquake, a mighty wind, and fire—great destructive forces. Elijah was overwhelmed by all three of those experiences, just like our feelings and our thoughts overwhelm us. Isn't that what your soul does? Soul makes noise and gets your attention. It diverts you. And if you think that's the deepest thing in you, you'll live according to it.

There was a paradox in the drama God staged for Elijah, however. God had said, "I am going to pass by you," but after every one of those events the Bible says, "but God wasn't in it." Three times God said, "I'm going to pass by you," but God wasn't in it.

Why did God stage a drama with such powerful forces only to be absent from them Himself? I saw that the Lord was saying to Elijah, "Everything in your life is ultimately of Me, Elijah. I've set the whole operation in motion, and I've kicked your swing into action. Nothing happens that I'm not active in, including your soul's feelings and thoughts. I take the messes that you or the devil make in your life and change them into discipline or some other blessing. So I'm a part of these outer things in your life, including your soul fluctuations. But I'm not in them, not in the deepest sense. I use them, but they are not Me. They are not the deepest understanding of Me you can have. You're going to miss Me, Elijah, if that's the deepest you can go."

That means we don't have to grab hold of that swing and stop it. We don't have to say, "I shouldn't have this feeling" or "I shouldn't have this thought." We don't have to play that game anymore. We don't have to go around denying us. We can accept our soul's fluctuations as something God is involved in and God intends. But God says, "If you judge reality by what's happening at your soul level, what you see and think and feel, you're going to miss Me."

The Scripture continues, saying that Elijah then heard "a still small voice." That's how the New King James Bible translates it. Other versions say "a soft, gentle blowing," or "sheer silence." I think it's an idea that's almost untranslatable. Looking at all the different translations and how they express it, I think we could best say that Elijah didn't hear anything. But though he hadn't heard anything audible, Elijah knew that he was in the presence of God. He took his mantle and wrapped it over his face.

I believe God was saying, "This is how I talk to you, Elijah. I don't talk to you in all that noise. I speak to your spirit in silence." That still small voice wasn't making any noise compared to those great disturbances. But in the stillness, in the silence, Elijah knew he was in the presence of God. That's how it is when spirit meets Spirit.

May the Holy Spirit show us the difference between the noise of the soul and the quietness of spirit. May He show us what it means to know spirit so we won't be confused and controlled by our feelings and our thoughts, but instead live in the rest that He has promised us.

Part Three

Who Are You?

8

One Nature

There's a deep rut in the Christian faith, as most believers experience it. It's like a ditch you run your car into and can't get out of. Unless God tows a believer out of the rut, he or she will never fully live out of their union with Christ.

The rut is this: most of us believe that in the depths of our being we are both good and bad. Or, to put it in theological terms, we are both righteous and sinful. Using a common illustration, we believe that we have within us both a white dog and a black dog, a good nature and a bad nature, both fighting for control.

But that's not true. It's vital that we know it's not true, because if we believe that we're both righteous and sinful, it will be impossible to live out of our union with Christ and to rest, trusting that He lives through us moment by moment. Instead, we will be focused on ourselves, on getting our act together, on winning the war supposedly raging within us, trying to suppress the bad part of us so that the good part will reflect the character of Christ. This endless self-effort is the complete opposite of what Paul wrote:

> I have been crucified with Christ; and it is no longer I who live, but Christ lives in me; and the life which I now live in the flesh I live by faith in the Son of God (Galatians 2:20).

The only way out of this dilemma of believing that we are both good and bad is to understand that the realm of the spirit, above the line, is singular. It is one. The realm of appearances, below the line, is a duality. It is two.

In the realm of appearances, there is constant evidence of good and evil, both outside and inside us. If we judge by appearances, we arrive at the logical conclusion that we are both good and bad. That looks entirely valid.

Christians have believed this for centuries. Except for a small minority who have come to know their true identity in Christ, the whole Christian world accepts this lie. Unfortunately, although something may not be true above the line, if below the line we think it is true, it still controls us. We must choose to live out of what is singular rather than what is dual.

The realm of the spirit, the singular realm, is eternal reality. That's where our spirit being lives and where our true identity is settled forever. Although we must live in the realm of appearance in the here and now, below the line, it is false as far as our identity goes. All of life depends on which realm is ultimate reality to you: the realm of spirit or the realm of appearances. That's going to determine what you believe and how you live.

Choosing to believe that you are not both good and evil can be difficult. All the external proof, all the apparent evidence, all the sight, supports the opposite: that you have two natures. "You are good, yes, a little good, but boy, you are still wicked too." Only the Holy Spirit can reveal to you that you have only one nature, not two. In the core of your being you are not both righteous and sinful; you are only righteous.

I want to take you through the Scriptures and allow the Holy Spirit to reveal this to you. I think you'll see that what we've been taught—that we have two natures—can't be true. But at the same time we can understand how we could believe that it is true, because of our experience. The question we're asking is: Who are you? Or we could say: Whom are you an expression of?

Scripture uses the word *nature* only two times in the way I'm using it, to describe who you really are. Ephesians 2:3 tells us that when we were born into the world we were "by nature children of wrath." Second

Peter 1:4 says that as believers we are "partakers of the divine nature." So do the Scriptures indicate that we are now both children of wrath and partakers of the divine nature? Or are we partakers of the divine nature only? Let's go through the Bible and see.

In Genesis 2, two trees are in the Garden: the Tree of the Knowledge of Good and Evil and the Tree of Life. God provided two trees and then He set up the necessity of choice. But was it a choice of both/and or either/or? Which was it? It was a choice of either/or, wasn't it? Not both/and. Adam could choose to eat from one or the other, but not both.

Tree here equals *nature*. If you could have two natures—if you could partake of two trees—it would be both/and. But God doesn't offer both/and. The tree that man chose, he was going to express. He would either choose to eat from and express the Tree of Life (Christ) or the Tree of the Knowledge of Good and Evil (human independence). So God said, "Don't eat of the Tree of the Knowledge of Good and Evil; if you do, you will die." It wasn't just physical death; it was primarily spiritual death or separation from God.

If humanity had eaten from the Tree of Life, we would have taken life, God's life, into us initially. But we opted for the other tree. That tree not only produced death; it also introduced the whole realm of duality that exists below the line. Remember, we took from the Tree of the Knowledge of Good *and* Evil.

As we have seen, if you're a believer, in Christ's death you also died. Concerning this context, you died to having taken of and being an expression of the Tree of the Knowledge of Good and Evil. That didn't erase good and evil for you below the line. But it erased it for you in your inmost being or spirit. At that moment, you became alive to and received another nature, God's nature. Using Genesis language, you finally partook of the Tree of Life.

We are not an expression of both trees. God didn't set it up in the beginning as both/and. He set it up as either/or. In the beginning Adam became alive to the Tree of the Knowledge of Good and Evil and died to the Tree of Life. We inherited that from him. But through our new birth in Christ, we died to the former and were made alive to the latter. In our deepest being, we partake from only one Tree. We have only one nature.

In Matthew 6:24, Jesus spoke of two masters:

> "No one can serve two masters; for either he will hate the one
> and love the other, or he will be devoted to one and despise
> the other. You cannot serve God and wealth."

The context is about God and riches, but the principle is the same. How many masters are presented to us? Two. But is it both/and? Or is it either/or? It's either/or, isn't it? In choosing Christ, we have chosen a different point of origin, a different master.

Yes, we still occasionally sin; I'm not saying we never do anything wrong. But that's not the point. The point is who is your master? We who are believers all have to confess, "Christ is my Master." Evil isn't our master. If we do evil we hate it. If we do evil we are remorseful. That's because evil is foreign to who we really are.

Living again now in western Kentucky, I run into many people I knew when I was young. During my early twenties I had a friend in Hopkinsville. He was a saved boy but wasn't practicing it, and I was a lost boy and was practicing it. So he and I would go out together and do the same sinful things.

Not long ago we ran into each other and reminisced about that. He said he had been bothered every night when he went home and went to bed after our outings. He had done something that he hated. He was remorseful. Not to the point of repentance yet, but remorseful. But I did the same things and it never bothered me. It never punctured my nature, because my nature was saying, "Good for you!" But his nature was saying, "That's not me. That's not me."

Outwardly, he and I were doing the same things. You wouldn't have known who was a Christian and who wasn't by looking at our behavior. But inside he knew he was of God. Later, I found out I wasn't of God.

When I made a decision for Christ, people told me, "You just rededicated your life; we remember when you joined the church as an eleven-year-old boy."

I replied, "Yes, sir, I did join, but I was as lost as a golf ball in high weeds."

What is your point of origin? That's the key. We can have only one Master.

Paul used the master-slave relationship in Romans 6:12-23. There he described two types of slaves: slaves of sin and slaves of righteousness. The question is whose slave are you? To whom did you present yourself? We presented ourselves to Christ as our Master. Since we have done that, Paul said, in essence, "You really are dead to that old stuff; put it away from your life." That admonition can be fulfilled only if you know the reality of who you are and who your life is—Christ.

It's a devilish trick to say "put off, put off, put off" when you really don't know who you are. You think you're a duality, both good and bad. You're being told to put off something that you've been taught is one of your natures. You're not settled yet in who your nature really is. You still think you are two. And you get frustrated and think, *Why tell me to put off something that is natural for me to do? I've had this habit for years. Why tell me to put it off if it's my nature?* So you get mad at God. You think He's telling you to suppress part of your true self. It's all because you don't know yet who you truly are.

You have only one nature. It's natural for you to put off sin, because sin is not your nature. You are already dead to it.

In John 8, Jesus clashed with the Pharisees. He told them,

> "You are doing the deeds of your father…You are of your
> father the devil, and you want to do the desires of your father"
> (8:41,44).

By contrast, Jesus repeatedly said things like, "I only do what I see with My Father."

The ones actually doing the deeds of the devil were saying to Jesus, "You've got the devil." They were judging by their interpretation of appearances. Jesus lived as one with the Father, but in the Pharisees' eyes He was breaking their religious rules. Jesus claiming to be one with the Father was blasphemy to them.

Do you see why it seems so logical to believe the wrong message? In the seen and temporal realm you are what you look like or act like. But in the unseen and eternal realm, you are what you were spiritually born as. We are born of God (1 John 5:1). God's Spirit gave birth to our spirit (John 3:3-6). We can't be both born of God and born of the devil. We can have only one father, not two.

In Romans 5:12-21, Paul wrote of two Adams. There is the first Adam:

> just as through one man sin entered into the world, and death
> through sin, and so death spread to all men, because all sinned
> (5:12).

And there is the last Adam, Jesus Christ:

> For if by the transgression of the one the many died, much
> more did the grace of God and the gift by the grace of the one
> Man, Jesus Christ, abound to the many (5:15).

From God's perspective, all of humanity is either in Adam or in Christ. Each is the head of a separate race of humans, spiritually. Tying back to Genesis 2, the first Adam represents the Tree of the Knowledge of Good and Evil, and the last Adam is the Tree of Life.

But we are not of them both. We are of either one or the other. We are either "in Adam" or "in Christ." The Bible never portrays humans as being in both simultaneously. It's impossible. But if you don't know by revelation that you are one, not two, it's perfectly logical to believe that you are both. That's because you only see how you act and feel and think, and to yourself you look like two. But you are not. You are one. As a believer you can be only in Christ.

In Romans 7:1-6, Paul discussed two husbands. The woman is bound by law to the first husband as long as he lives. But if the husband dies, she is released and can marry whomever she wants to. But she can be married to only one at a time.

Paul was drawing an analogy. He explained that we were married to the law, but when we died on the cross, we died to our first husband and were released from him. We died to the law. We died to the Tree of the Knowledge of Good and Evil. We died to that first Adam who had been expressing himself through us. Now we have a new Husband. We are married to Christ, and we are going to express the life of the Husband we have intimacy with, that we are joined to, that we are the expression of.

Our human gender, male or female, doesn't matter here. In our spirit, we are all joined to one husband or the other. If we slip out one night and go back to the first husband, what have we committed? Adultery. If we produce an offspring, an act or a deed from that adulterous relationship, that's an illegitimate child. The real husband can't acknowledge that child. It's not his child.

The point is this: You can't have two husbands. You either have one or the other. You can't have two at the same time. It's illegal!

We could make the exact same point from Paul in Romans 9. There are two types of vessels: vessels of wrath and vessels of mercy. You're one or the other. But not both. You can't be both!

The same truth continues in John's first letter:

> By this you know the Spirit of God: every spirit that confesses that Jesus Christ has come in the flesh is from God; and every spirit that does not confess Jesus is not from God; this is the spirit of the antichrist…You are from God, little children, and have overcome them; because greater is He who is in you than he who is in the world (1 John 4:2-4).

There are two spirits. One spirit confesses Jesus Christ. One doesn't. Of which spirit are you? We confess that Jesus Christ is the Son of God. If ever you are in doubt about your true identity, this is a good place to return: whom do you truly confess? Somebody presses in on you, gets past the external stuff you're in, and asks you the truth—"To whom do you belong? Whom do you confess?" No matter what mess you're in, if you're honest you have to say, "I belong to Christ. I may not be proud of how I'm acting right now, but I belong to Christ." You are of only one spirit, not two.

I'm not denying that in the realm you and I live in, below the line, there are two possibilities. We can do good or evil. There's no sense arguing about that. But we don't just live in the seen and temporal. That's not where our identity comes from. We are spirit beings. As spirit beings, we cannot be both good and evil. We need to see, if we haven't already, that we can be only one expression of a tree; we can have only one master; we can have only one father; we can have only one husband; we can be only one type of vessel; we can be only of one spirit. We can be only one!

The teaching on two natures is so persuasive because it looks true. In the realm of experience, you feel it and you think it. So what keeps it from being true? The fact that you are not who you think or feel. You are who God says you are. And God says you are holy. You are righteous. You are blameless.

So why do we look like we have two natures? Because the power of sin is alive and well in us—but not in our inner man, our true identity. Paul explains that our inner man is now on God's side, but the members of our body are not:

> For I joyfully concur with the law of God in the inner man,
> but I see a different law in the members of my body, waging
> war against the law of my mind, and making me a prisoner
> of the law of sin which is in my members (Romans 7:22-23).

So sin is alive and well in us. But where is it? In the members of our body, Paul says. We have a new spirit, born of the Holy Spirit, but we still live in unredeemed bodies that have been programmed to sin. So we will have to deal with the power of sin until we eject out of these bodies. (God uses that continuing tension in us for our good, as we will see in chapter 18.)

But for our purposes now it's vital to see this: no matter how much we think according to it, feel according to it, or act according to it, the power of sin in our bodies is not us. Paul makes that clear:

> But if I do the very thing I do not wish to do, I agree with the
> Law, confessing that it is good. So now, no longer am I the
> one doing it, but sin which indwells me (Romans 7:16-17).

Just to make sure his readers didn't miss it, he says it again three verses later:

> But if I am doing the very thing I do not want, I am no longer
> the one doing it, but sin which dwells in me (7:20).

God draws an impenetrable wall between sin and the true you. God knows you are on one side of that wall and sin is on the other. He knows that while you still do sin, you are not a sinner at heart. You are a saint, His beloved child whom He birthed.

Two illustrations can drive this home for us. If I handed you a certificate and said, "By signing this certificate, you will be guaranteed never to sin again," would you sign it? If you're a child of God you would because that's your heart: to do the will of your Father. But good luck trying to find an unregenerate person who would sign it. Their heart is for themselves, not God.

Or take that previous illustration about adultery. Let's say you're married to Mr. Jones, but tonight you're going to slip out and act like Mrs. Baker. So you go out with Mr. Baker and act like Mrs. Baker tonight. He may introduce you as Mrs. Baker and the two of you may pretend as though you are Mr. and Mrs. Baker all night long. But are you? Pretending doesn't make it so. Acting like it doesn't make it so. There's nothing written in the heavens that makes it so. You are Mrs. Jones, regardless of how you act that night. But the evil one wants to keep our attention on how we act so that we might identify ourselves according to our behavior.

It's easy to see why we can be fooled into thinking we are a duality, having two natures. But we became a singularity the moment we received the nature of Jesus Christ as our nature. We were one nature, not two. We just didn't know it. We were the expression of one, the One who gave birth to us. We won't operate consistently out of that one nature, however, unless we know it. Until then, we will express our true nature from time to time—we can't help expressing some of God's life within us—but it won't be consistent.

The two-nature belief results in misery. It puts us right back in Romans 7: "The good I want to do, I don't do, and the evil I don't want to do, I do. Oh, miserable person that I am, who shall deliver me?"

That's where most of us have found ourselves, trying to beat down one of these masters and help the other one to ascend. Who was in control of that? We were. We were trying to do that. As I said before, this leads to nothing but endless self-effort and failure. And then the answer finally comes: Christ is my life!

The soul is forever trapped in duality. It looks good one day, bad the next. Only the spirit is single. It is either righteous or sinful, not both. Unbelievers are not both righteous and sinful. In the depths of their being, in their spirit, they are sinful (Ephesians 2:1-3). Doing a good deed doesn't make them righteous. Likewise, doing a bad deed doesn't make you sinful.

God's nature within us is single. His nature is our nature. God crucified our old nature (Romans 6:6) and imparted to us a new righteous one. But we won't know this without a revelation from the Holy Spirit, because everything in this seen and temporal realm supports the lie that you have two natures.

May God deepen our understanding of what He has already done, revealing to us that our old self is truly dead and that we truly are His righteous, holy children.

9

The Real You

We are born into a tough existence. As infants, every day is a new challenge to ensure all our needs are met. Before we are even aware of it, we learn to play the world's game of life. We learn that if we cry, we get attention. We don't get any attention sleeping all day long and being good. By making noise, we get fed, dried, changed, and played with.

It isn't much longer before we learn that if we behave a certain way, Momma and Daddy like that, and if we behave another way, they don't like it. We discover there may be punishment involved if we misbehave, but if we behave properly, there are rewards. So we conclude, *I'd better not do that. I'd better do this.*

We start school. We learn, *If I act like this, the teacher likes me. If I act like that, she doesn't like me. So I'd better act like this instead of like that.* Going through school, if we have a personality that others are attracted to, we become one of the most popular kids in school. We learn how to operate in that. If we're not popular, we learn how to live with that. In high school, if we have a boyfriend or girlfriend, we learn how to adapt to that or we learn how to get along without it.

When we get into the work world, we learn what will earn us advancement and what will earn us the pink slip. Then we get married and we think we're going to live happily ever after. It's God's trick. Marriage is meant to press you into Him, not to provide you bliss. If you happen to find bliss, it's not permanent. Marriage isn't like that for most people. Marriage is for discovering real intimacy.

It's all a rat maze. We try to nose our way into some place of stability where we can exist and get along. We're constantly learning, reacting, and making adjustments to do what it takes to make it in the world. From the moment we were born into the world dead in trespasses and sins—dead in spirit, separated from God—the world and the devil conspired to create this self in us that could try independently to get along. It's what I call the false self.

The Bible calls the false self "flesh." But flesh carries a negative connotation that can mislead us as to its real meaning. Paul wrote to the Galatians: "Now the deeds of the flesh are evident, which are: immorality, impurity, sensuality, idolatry, sorcery, enmities, strife…" and a whole bunch of other bad things (5:19-21). That's true, of course. The flesh does produce those things. But the flesh can produce plenty of things that look perfectly acceptable on the outside, such as self-reliance, dependability, self-discipline, and so on. The flesh, or the false self, is simply the body and the soul operating apart from the Holy Spirit.

The false self is a soul-based self. It's the soul operating independently of its Source. I don't want to minimize the vital role of the soul in God's economy. The life of God through us must be expressed through the soul. But His life is expressed through a soul dependent upon its Source, not acting independently of it.

As an unbeliever our spirit was dead to God, so we became dominated by our soul (*psychē* in Greek). Our soul was turned toward the world, getting its direction and validation from the external environment. We were a natural man, as Paul called it, living a soul-based life.

Somewhere along the way we got saved and our sins were forgiven. And we wanted to live this thing called the Christian life, but we didn't know how to live out of our new spirit. So we fell back upon our only other resource: the false self. It knew how to get along in the world. We just made a few adjustments to fit the Christian scene. We were sitting ducks for the how-to books, which told us how to manipulate the false self to make it more effective in getting along.

Although having the Holy Spirit in our spirit, we didn't know about the Holy Spirit living the life of Christ through us. So our mode of operation was the same as for the unbeliever: self-reliance. That's what the false self is: our attempt to independently operate our own lives. As Christians, the false self even tries to do it for the glory of God.

This created realm has played such an important part in our lives that it's hard for us as believers to change our perspective about ourselves. It's hard to stop viewing our humanity—and I'm not using humanity here in a negative sense but in a neutral one—as the most important thing about us. It's not. We view other people's humanity as the most important thing about them too. It's not. We see our humanity as all-important until we come to know Christ not just as the forgiver of our sins but as our life. Then the One within us becomes all-important. Until then, our focus is constantly on ourselves: how we are performing, how we are appearing, how we are growing, how we are measuring up. Paul addressed this issue with the Corinthians:

> For the love of Christ controls us, having concluded this, that one died for all, therefore all died; and He died for all, so that they who live might no longer live for themselves, but for Him who died and rose again on their behalf.
>
> Therefore from now on we recognize no man according to the flesh; even though we have known Christ according to the flesh, yet now we know Him in this way no longer (2 Corinthians 5:14-16).

Paul says we once knew the human Jesus, but we don't regard Him that way anymore. Not that we disregard His humanity, but we are no longer fixated on the historical, human Jesus, who lived in the seen and temporal realm. Our emphasis is on the eternal, indwelling Christ. That is how we regard Christ. That is how we regard others. And that is how we regard ourselves. Paul continues:

> Therefore if anyone is in Christ, he is a new creation; old things have passed away; behold, all things have become new. Now all things are from God… (5:17-18a, NKJV).

Are you in Christ? If so, you are a new creation. At your new birth, God birthed in you a new spirit, created in His likeness, in holiness and righteousness (Ezekiel 36:26; John 3:6-8; Ephesians 4:24).

I like what David Needham says in *Birthright*: at that moment a new person came into being who had never existed before. You are not a repaint job but a brand new creature. The old you was crucified on the cross with Christ. The new you was born of the Holy Spirit and has been raised with Christ and seated with Him in the heavenlies (Ephesians 2:6). You were dead spiritually; now you are alive spiritually. For the first time you are alive the way God meant you to be alive. In your spirit you are a completely new creation.

Do you look like a new creation? No. You look like the same old Tom, Dick, Harry, Mary, Jane, or Elizabeth. Externally, you still are. But you have been renewed from within. Life is within. What you've been trying to bring into being below the line, Paul says you already are. You already are a new creature. You don't have to try to become a new creature. But you're going to try to become a new creature until you know you're a new creature.

Of course, we can give mental assent: "Yes, I'm a new creature, but…"

Where you're really living is going to be determined by what you put after the *but*. "I'm a new creature, but…"

But what?

"But I sure do fail a lot."

Then that's the way you see yourself. You don't see yourself as a new creature. You see yourself as someone who fails a lot. Instead, you could say, "I sure do fail a lot, but I'm a new creature." Then that's where you're living. You're always living after the *but*.

You're a new creation in Christ Jesus. The old is gone. Gone to whom? To God. It may not disappear as quickly to you as you'd like in the seen and temporal realm, but it's gone to God. He sees the unseen and eternal. He sees the first from the last. And He knows that the old is gone. The question is who's keeping score? You or God? The old you is gone to the One who is in charge of the universe. To Him, you aren't the same person you were before you entered into Christ. You're a brand new creation in Christ.

It took me more than 20 years after getting saved to catch up to what I already was. I said, "Oh, my goodness. Look how God has been seeing me all these years, and I've been bogged down in this flesh conflict, continually trying to make myself new, and losing." The losing ceased when I stopped trying to *become* who I wanted to be and saw that I already *was*.

God has a different point of reference for us than we do. He doesn't fasten His attention on our flesh or false self. He doesn't fasten His attention on our soul, our *psychē*. He looks at us from a different reference point. He looks at the new creation that His Spirit gave birth to. Paul wrote to the Corinthians:

> [The Father] made Him [Jesus] who knew no sin to be sin on our behalf, so that we might become the righteousness of God in Him (2 Corinthians 5:21).

Jesus was made sin for us, and when He as sin died, we as sinners died. When He as the Righteous One of God was raised, we as the righteousness of God were raised with Him. He has made us to be His righteousness. To God, you are as though you've never sinned. To the Ephesians, Paul explained:

> He chose us in Him before the foundation of the world, that we would be holy and blameless before Him (1:4).

To the Colossians he wrote:

> He has now reconciled you in His fleshly body through death, in order to present you before Him holy and blameless and beyond reproach (1:22).

That is a righteous person. Of no unrighteous person could that be spoken. You're not waiting to become holy and blameless and beyond reproach. God sees as you holy and blameless and beyond reproach before Him right now. When He looks at you, He sees the nature of His Son. He sees you as love. He sees you as joy. He sees you as peace. He sees you as righteous. He sees you redeemed. He sees you justified. He sees you perfect. He sees you complete.

> For in [Christ] all the fullness of deity dwells in bodily form, and in Him you have been made complete (Colossians 2:9-10a).

The word *complete* carries the idea of fully mature. That's in the unseen and eternal realm. This is the way God sees you: complete, fully mature. You are not only accepted by God, you are acceptable to Him.

This is the real you. Your false self—your flesh and its independent efforts to cope in the world—is not the real you. The real you is a new creation: righteous, holy, blameless, acceptable, and beloved.

It's an affront to God to keep talking about how unworthy we are. It's a statement of unbelief. "I really don't believe what God says about me; I believe what I think about me." We're never going to get anywhere that way. It isn't being humble. It's a false humility. It's the teaching of tradition and the flesh, because it appears humble.

What's truly humble is agreeing with what God says about you. Nothing more. Nothing less. We are the righteousness of God. We don't look it all the time. We don't feel it all the time. We don't think it all the time. But we are.

Knowing our true identity brings us many benefits, two of which I especially want to highlight. First, knowing our true identity gives us a deep awareness of this vital truth: *there isn't any condemnation for us*. Paul said it straight out in Romans 8:1:

> There is now no condemnation for those who are in Christ
> Jesus.

There is no condemnation from God. There is to be no condemnation from ourselves either. If you want to take condemnation, you have perfect liberty to take it. But in Christ there is no condemnation. The evil one and the world try to put condemnation on us. "You're no good. Remember that promise you made to God? You're not keeping it." We do a pretty good job of heaping condemnation on ourselves as well. But there is no condemnation, so don't take it. Tell the devil to beat it. "I don't have any more dealings with you. Regardless of what I am thinking or feeling or what I just did, I am not condemned. I am the righteousness of God in Christ."

As we grow spiritually, we learn the difference between the Spirit's voice and the evil one's voice. The Spirit never witnesses to your spirit in condemnation.

He might give you a check sometimes: "Wait a minute. Wait a minute." But not in condemnation. He might tell you you're wrong sometimes. But not in condemnation. He rebukes, He corrects, He points out, but He never condemns. He wants to build you up, to undergird you, to increase your understanding of the life of God in you. He wants you to see how God already sees you. You are a saint, a holy one. You are blameless. You are beyond reproach.

The great release is understanding that we are never condemned. Anytime we feel condemned, we can return without a moment's notice to who we really are.

Knowing our true identity provides a second vital benefit: it enables us to live with a Christ-consciousness instead of a sin-consciousness. God doesn't want us living with a sin-consciousness. On occasion someone will ask me if I still sin. I answer, "I don't know. I'm not paying any attention." I mostly say that to get their attention. But truthfully, the only way you can answer a spiritual inventory question is to be watching yourself. You have to be preoccupied with you instead of God. You have to be preoccupied with below the line instead of above the line.

To be sin-conscious is to be sin-centered. The writer to the Hebrews explained that Jesus came to deliver us from sin-consciousness:

> For the Law…can never, by the same sacrifices…year by year, make perfect those who draw near. Otherwise, would they not have ceased to be offered, because the worshipers, having once been cleansed, would no longer have had consciousness of sins? But in those sacrifices there is a reminder of sins year by year…
>
> [But] by [Christ's] one offering [God] has perfected for all time those who are sanctified (10:1-3,14).

God did not intend for humanity to live with a sin-consciousness but with a God-consciousness. He doesn't intend for us to live with a self-consciousness but with a Christ-in-us consciousness. Does that mean we ignore it when the Holy Spirit wants to point out sin to us? Of course not. But it means we let Him do the pointing rather than us constantly looking for or assuming the presence of sin.

We are saints, not sinners. We need to live with that awareness. Most Christians love to talk about what horrible sinners they are. Not to God they aren't. I was talking to two deacons (both fine men) in our church one night. I said, "I want to ask you something. Why do you always pray, 'Forgive us of our sins.'"

They thought and said, "Well, we always do that."

"I know you always do it, but why do you do it?"

"Well, it just seems like we ought to."

"Did the Holy Spirit say you had done anything bad?" I asked.

"Well...no."

"Then let's agree to have a moratorium around here on asking to be forgiven for sins until the Holy Spirit says, 'You just blew it.' Then ask to be forgiven. But don't even ask to be forgiven. Rejoice in the Lord that you are forgiven. Just rejoice in the Lord that you are, because He's already taken that one to the cross, hasn't He? Did He leave one out that He didn't know you were going to do? No. He's already taken it there."

When we fail to live out of our true identity (our true self), we are living out of our flesh (our false self). We are then living with ourselves as our reference point. We are choosing not to acknowledge who we really are and who Christ is in us. We are choosing not to act like who we really are. That's a dangerous place to live. It's not real life; it's a fake. There's only one source you can truly live from, and that's God, your spiritual marriage partner, whom you are in union with. He's the only One who gives you your true identity.

Our true identity is not in the externals. It's not in our performance. Our false self's identity is in the externals, but our true identity is not. Jesus said,

> "Whoever wishes to save his life will lose it, but whoever loses his life for My sake, he is the one who will save it" (Luke 9:24).

We read that verse in English and can assume Jesus is talking about our physical life. But He isn't. The Greek word translated "life" is *psychē*—soul. Jesus is saying, "If you hold on to this soul-life, this false self, you're going to lose real life. But if you're willing to lose this soul-life, not be dominated by the soul-life, not live according to the false self, you will gain life."

Living in the soul-life is always the temptation. Being a pastor, I was prone to live in a religious soul-life. I drew my identity from religious externals. They looked good and proper and seemed like a worthwhile thing to draw my identity from. It's hard to avoid that trap. There's nothing wrong with being involved in the religious world if it's not giving you your identity. If it is, it's an idol. It's telling you something external about yourself. But we can truthfully say, "I'm not an external person. I'm an internal person who does some external things. But I'm not doing these external things to tell me who I am."

Any activity that's giving you your identity is an idol and is contributing only to the false self. Our false self thinks it needs external things or activities to give it life. It wants the stroking, the external affirmation, the place of authority, or the public place to make pronouncements. We are dangerous living out of our flesh, because we're using others to validate us. But when we no longer need those externals—when who we are in Christ and who He is in us has become foundational truth in our life—then we can handle the externals because we don't need them for our identity.

God will take us through situations again and again to bring us to the place where He is our total life, where we are living out of our true identity. Once we are, He can give us back the external things. He put me back in the world of religion. At that point I was safe there, because it had ceased to be a place of identity for me. It was simply a place of service, where His life was to be poured out through me for others.

We are spirit beings. We are the precious means by which the Father reproduces His life. We are the righteousness of God in Christ. We are God-lovers. We are not our job or our ministry or our children or our possessions. We are not our false self, and we don't have to constantly manipulate our false self, trying to improve it or make it look good.

Our culture is obsessed with improving the false self, teaching us to cope better. Certainly there is much that can be done to help the false self, to help it look better or manage better. But all of these efforts to change the false self will never lead to godliness. The answer to the false self is not more effort. When God reveals Himself to us, we see the things freely given to us. We've been given a new life. Christ is our life.

Let's get on with God. Let's get on with the life of the Spirit. I don't mean to discredit what the fields of psychiatry and psychology do in the area they work in, but God wants us to push beyond the psyche—which is what they deal with—and on to the spirit, which is what God primarily deals with. God wants us to develop the life of the spirit within us.

I can't rule out what Almighty God may do for someone through means other than the route He has taken me. Helping the soul is the way many want to go, including a lot of people who need immediate help, and often their immediate situation can be helped. But I'm emphasizing the realm God has given me to teach: the realm of the Spirit and the spirit, of God living in you and through you and bringing spiritual healing to you.

When you start with the spirit, spiritual healing can filter into the other areas of your life. God did that in my life. He may yet have a lot more to do, but He has done that. Perhaps I could have benefited by other ways of approaching my life situation, but when I did have a crisis, I didn't go to a counselor. In my soul I was mad at God, but in my spirit I wasn't. That's because His Spirit was already joined to my spirit, whether I knew it or not. So I just wrestled the thing out with Him.

Another route may have revealed more about my upbringing, why I was like I was. I already knew most of that anyway. I'm sure there were deeper things going on than I knew about, but by saying, "I'll just wrestle this out with God," what I laid hold of was spirit reality. That was the way God wanted me to go: the way of my true self. Ultimately, He wants us all to go the way of our true self.

Our true self is who we are at the spirit level. At the deepest level of your personhood you are not a sinner. You are a saint. You are God's holy, righteous, blameless child. You have His nature. In your deepest personhood, your desires are not in conflict with God's will. Your deepest being always wants to do your Father's will, just as Jesus wanted to do His Father's will (Romans 7:22; John 4:34).

This is your eternal, changeless identity. This is who you are. That you experience thoughts and feelings and even behavior to the contrary does not change that fact. Only by accepting this by faith can we begin to experience its reality.

If we haven't received this understanding, then one thing ought to be occupying our time and attention: the prayer request, "Father, I want to receive the understanding of who I really am in Christ. I do receive it in faith and I want to receive it in experience." That's the preeminent prayer if you are in that place. That's been the prayer of everyone who now knows who he or she is and has learned to live out of it.

10

God's Precious Assets

If we want to begin to operate our lives from the unseen and eternal realm, we have to put ourselves on the shelf. This life won't work until you get yourself out of the way. You get yourself out of the way simply by believing this: *You are not a liability to God. You are His precious asset.*

As long as you live under the false idea that you are a liability to God, then no matter how things are going, you will feel inadequate. You will feel that you come up short and are not all that God wants you to be. You will constantly be focused on trying to get your act together. Until you see that you are already all God wants you to be—that you are an asset to God, not a liability—then you will never be established in the fact that living waters are flowing out through you. But when you finally make peace with who you are, you can begin to experience the realm of life God has destined you for.

When we died on the cross, we permanently died to being a liability to God. From His point of view, we can no longer be a liability. Even if we're messing up we're not a liability because He's going to use it somehow in our life or in somebody else's life, or both. Until we came to Christ we were nothing but a liability. And the better we were on the outside, the more of a liability we were because we esteemed our own righteousness.

Foundational truth is to know you died with Christ and that you are no longer a liability. Having been raised with Christ, you can no longer be anything to God but an asset. He has accepted you. He is pleased with you. He uses you, lives through you, speaks through you, loves through you.

Our humanity is God's asset. If we are meant to function on the human level—which is how God made us—we can't deny our humanity. We don't like things we think and feel, so we want to reject our humanness. But our humanity has to be part of God's plan; otherwise, how can we express Him? He has designed us to express Him through our humanity. So denial of our humanity isn't the answer.

The union of the human spirit and the Divine Spirit needs a way to express itself. Our soul and body are the means by which God expresses His union with our spirit. So our humanity comes very much into play. Our feelings and thoughts have to be involved in the process or we can't be true expressers.

Radio broadcasting illustrates this truth. Unless you're living in Outer Mongolia (and perhaps even there), all kinds of programs are being broadcast around you right now. But if you don't have your radio turned on, you're not getting any of them. The radio in your house or car is the means by which the broadcast is manifested. Spirit is like radio programming. It's out there, but it has no point of contact unless there is a vehicle to receive it and express it. Without a point of contact, it can't be expressed. You—your humanity—are God's point of contact.

God joined to you, one spirit, is absolute, bedrock truth. But God expresses Himself through the total you. Spirit, soul, *and* body is the means of His expression. You can't even talk without a body. It's impossible. The total you is involved in speaking: your mind, your emotions, your will, your mouth, your vocal cords. We are a total person. We express Him as total people. God says to us, "I'm going to live in you, and other people are going to see you, but you know it's Me."

What this tells us is that we can stop seeing ourselves as a liability. We can cease thinking that something more needs to happen to us spiritually before we can be an asset to God. If we keep focusing on ourselves externally, we'll keep thinking, *He can't use me yet.* If we focus on Christ living in us, we can put ourselves on the shelf as a liability and begin to see ourselves as an asset.

If we're in union with God, then He must have *us* to express Himself through. (I'm not saying we're indispensable; I'm saying this is how God has chosen to operate.) So if we are a necessary part of both God's eternal plan and His plan in the here and now, we're not a liability. We're an asset. Our function is to be in union with the Greater and let Him express Himself through the lesser. We are vessels—containers of the life of God. But we are not the contents of the vessel. God is. We cannot produce His life. We can only express it.

Do you want to see what it's like for a vessel to try to be the contents? Take a bite out of a Styrofoam cup and start chewing on it. It doesn't taste very good. That's what happens when the vessel tries to give itself away rather than its contents. The cup doesn't taste as good as lemonade or coffee or Coke. But it's what we get if we start chewing the external, looking for the eternal.

Paul explained our role as God's assets this way: "We have this treasure [the life of Jesus] in earthen vessels, so that the surpassing greatness of the power will be of God and not from ourselves" (2 Corinthians 4:7).

We are earthen vessels. We have this treasure in *earthen* vessels. The beauty of the vessel is its content. The frustration is when the vessel tries to become the contents. When we reduce the illustration to that, we see how silly it is to try to be the contents. If you became the contents, there wouldn't be any vessel to hold you. You can't be both the vessel holding (expressing) the life of God and at the same time try to be the life of God. Only He is the life. Only He can live the life through you.

Your eternal purpose isn't to become the contents of the cup. Your eternal purpose is to be the vessel, to let the life flow out of you. Then you will say, "I only do what I see with Christ. I only speak what I hear with Christ."

People will reply, "Well, it sure did look like you. It sure did sound like you."

Because you know the truth, that it's really the life of Christ in you, you can say, "Thank you." If you don't know the truth, you'll go back home and exclaim, "Someone recognized me. Someone saw that I'm a Christian. Someone saw what I did!"

God said, "Let us make man in Our image." We are not the essence of God but the image of the essence. We are the mirror of the essence, the means of the essence. We reflect the glory and the nature of the One we contain. God manifests Himself to people through people. He first did it through the God-Man, Jesus. He does it now through us.

Being an earthen vessel is more than just being a clay pot. It's a beautiful union of giver and receiver and expresser. It raises us to the level of our original purpose. Even after the fall of man, God's original intent never changed. God intended that we would come to the place where we say, "I am the image of the invisible God. I am the means by which the invisible God manifests Himself."

I can't be anything but a receiver and a manifestor of the Person I'm in union with. If that's all I can do, that's not hard to do. If that's all I can be, that's not hard to be. It's not hard to be Dan Stone. But if I am trying to be somebody else, that is most difficult.

When I was about 10 years old, a local athlete who was 18 became my idol. He had the weirdest walk you ever saw. He was a fairly short fellow, but he had a big, long step and walked bent over. When I began to bend over and take an extended step, my mom and dad said, "What are you walking like him for? That isn't you. That's not natural." Well, I got over that and started walking normally again. It wasn't easy to act unnaturally, trying to emulate my idol. But it was easy to be just me. In the same way, if I know that I'm just meant to be me—not the originator of the life but the means by which the life is manifested—then that's easy.

Living the life as God's asset has an ease to it. But it's an inner ease. The rest for the soul is not lying in a hammock 24 hours a day. The rest for our soul lies in the reality of the spirit. We operate out of the reality of spirit joined to Spirit, where the two join to accomplish the purposes of the One. We operate from this inner Person, who is able to do through us, as us, what pleases Him. Previously, we could only try to do what we thought would please Him and offer that to Him. One was laborious, frustrating work. The other is easy.

I've emphasized how God made us new creations at our new birth. That is rock-bottom truth. In a sense, though, you have the same humanity now that you had before. Your spirit is new, but you didn't receive a new personality the moment you received Christ. You're still mostly outgoing or reserved, spontaneous or deliberate. Your humanity is basically the same before and after. But can you accept it now? Can you even glory in it now?

If your mechanic puts a new engine in your car, can you glory in your car even though it still has rust spots? Yes, you can. And that's what God is saying to us. "If I am willing to put a new engine in your car and glory in your car, will you glory with Me?"

That's one of the hardest lessons we have to learn: to glory in our humanity. To be satisfied with ourselves as we are. Is there a harder lesson? Every one of us has something about our humanity—our personality or our body—that we wish God would change so that we'd look better for Him, at least from our perspective. We think, *God, if you'd just take that thing away, I'd look better for You.* That "thing" may be with us until they plant us six feet under.

My "thing" has been the same for years. It probably will be for years to come. "Lord, why don't you make me patient? I'd look so much better for You if You'd just take away my impatience."

When I was still traveling around the country, it occurred to me that if I were too patient, I'd probably sit at home the rest of my life, because I'm a pretty lazy fellow. It doesn't take the expense of much energy to satisfy me. But I'd be home a few weeks and I'd get impatient. The restlessness I have while driving, for example—the restlessness in me that I find unpleasant—is the same restlessness God used to get me out on the road to go see someone, to go revisit a group, or to go share with a new group. What had been a curse was now a blessing because my perspective on it changed. I entrusted that part of my humanity to God.

People can relate to you through your warts and blemishes. They can't relate to your holiness. You're too slick there. You've got it too together. They can relate to your warts, though.

We come to a place where we say, "Lord, even though that thing is still in my humanity, I'm going to praise You for it." And you know what I discovered? The minute I started praising God for my impatience, I didn't see it anymore.

I don't mean it disappeared, but I didn't have a fixation on it. I wasn't anxious about it any longer. That's the way God moves on in us, when we accept ourselves as He does.

I'm not advocating sin, by any means. I am saying that when we shift our focus from ourselves—some neutral aspect of our personality that we don't like, or, yes, even some flesh pattern that keeps recurring—and instead focus on Christ in us, God does His work in us. We are transformed into His image as we behold Him, not as we behold ourselves (2 Corinthians 3:18).

God takes those things that are fixations in us when we're flesh-oriented and turns them into blessings when we're spirit-oriented. What I despised became a blessing in somebody else's life. Those things the locusts ate became the things God restored, the dung that God makes into a compost pile. He lets it sit there until it's done a work in us. Then we can take our humanity back and say, "It's perfect to God right now. If He wants to do any altering of it, He is at work in me to will and do of His good pleasure. If He wants to change it, He who began a good work in me will bring it to pass. He will finish what He started."

I'm not going to take my humanity back on my terms. I don't want it back that way. It took me long enough to get rid of it—as the source of my life. When you see it's no longer the starting point of your life, but rather the means by which God's life is manifested, then you can take it back. You can accept yourself as you are. You can accept yourself as God's asset.

Finally we're able to say, "Lord, through my family tree and all the circumstances I've come through, You've made the outer person that I am. You live in that person, and You set that person in the world in a way that's going to attract some people to You. I'm not going to attract everybody. The ones You don't attract through me, You'll catch through someone else."

That's why we all fit together, isn't it? We fit together into a whole. Nobody can attract everybody. I used to try to attract everybody. But there are all kinds of fruit. There are oranges. There are apples. There are lemons. God uses all kinds. I say to people, "I'm a lemon." God attracts some people through my lemonness.

You come to a place of inner peace, knowing that the warts—the imperfections—that constitute your outer humanity will be the very things some brother or sister, boy or girl will be able to get hold of. They'll be able to relate to that wart. And as they do, they'll receive the life that lives in you.

We don't have to be anybody else; we don't have to submit to anyone trying to make us like anybody else, either. We're free to be ourselves.

God is pleased to manifest His beautiful variety of expression through each of us in our uniqueness.

I was in New England for a couple of weeks one fall. Seeing the beautiful varieties of autumn color amazed me. Everyone was excited about the different colored leaves. But get among most Christians and they all want to be one color. They all want to be brown. Or blue. We walk out into the world and say, "Isn't God beautiful? Isn't it wonderful that He gave us all these colors?" We are grateful to God for His variety—until He comes to live in human beings. Then we say, "Better shape up. You're not acting like the rest of us."

That's the devil's trick, to say to us, "Since God is one, then all of you better be one too. You all have to look the same." We are one where it counts: in the inner man, our spirit. We are all made in His likeness and are one in the Spirit. But our inner oneness frees us to be variety on the outside. According to Paul, that's the way it should be in the Body of Christ. There will be different ministries because God is going to reveal to people different roles, such as apostle, prophet, evangelist, or pastor/teacher. Rather than trying to find something to do for God, we will have some role that God impresses upon our lives. We won't all be the same, but we'll all see the Spirit of God in us. That's part of standing fast in the liberty with which Christ has set us free, rather than regimenting everybody's activity and service to God.

Variety in ministry is part of us being God's precious assets, of God expressing His life through us in different ways. So is variety in relationships. We don't all have to have marriages, friendships, and other relationships that look the same. We are free to be different because all of these varieties are anchored in the inner person—who we truly are.

In our deepest being, the only person we are is *love,* in honor preferring one another. But we express that love—God's love—in manifold ways.

As earthen vessels, we are a variety of colors, sizes, shapes, appetites, interests, and energies. The bottom line is that we're always operating from what a friend of mine calls the Holy Wink: to others, it looks like us, but we know it's Christ in us. We are at peace in our spirit union with God, knowing that our outer humanity is God's perfect instrument. This is the means by which God touches the world.

Thank God for your humanity. Thank God for your parents, even for the difficult things you inherited from them. God used them to help make you the perfect instrument you are. Thank God for your warts. Praise God for them, because He's going to make them a blessing in somebody else's life. Take back your humanity as the dwelling place of the Most High God. Make peace with you. When the Holy Spirit showed me that it pleased God to live in me, then I had to be satisfied with me. God was.

Let it dawn on you that you are no longer a liability to God. You are a wonderful and beautiful and necessary asset. You are the vessel by which the world drinks. You are the means by which the world sees the love and life of God. As we rest in that, we move into a permanent position of being a faith person.

Part Four

Knowing God's Ways

11

Revelation: God's Way of Knowing

A few years ago a friend told me how he finally discovered by revelation—experientially—that he had been crucified with Christ. It was a shock to me because I had known this fellow for several years and we had batted these truths back and forth repeatedly. I thought he already knew that he had been crucified with Christ. But his own confession to me was, "No, I didn't. I really didn't know it. I talked it, but I didn't know it."

I appreciated that word from him because it underscored the process of knowing our union. For years I traveled around the country teaching people about our union with Christ. I would draw a few simple diagrams on the board, trying to give them something to hang on to so they could mentally see how things work. But after a while I discovered this: brain understanding is not spiritual understanding.

That's difficult for people to grasp because Western civilization processes everything mentally. We try to comprehend it with the head and get the head to tell it to the heart, instead of waiting for the Holy Spirit to tell it to the heart. If it's in the heart, we will know it. If it's in the head, we will just know about it. It's easy to get a handle on all of these union phrases and Christ-in-you clauses and get an outline all down pat and go around talking about it. But knowing *about* is not the same as knowing.

Everything we truly know of God comes by revelation of the Holy Spirit. The work of the Holy Spirit is to reveal to us the reality of the mysteries of God. These are in the unseen and eternal realm and as God's children they are our right to know, but only the Holy Spirit can tell us those realities. Until the Holy Spirit tells us, God's unseen and eternal realities seem to be outside of us. So we set out to gain information about them, thinking that if we gain enough information, we can then pro-duce the spiritual life. Some of us have garnered entire libraries to help us gain the spiritual life, as if it were an outside thing—a thing—to be gained by knowledge. Of course, what we ended up with was not much spiritual life but lots of information about it.

Unfortunately, there's no relationship between the amount of infor-mation we accumulate about the spiritual life and our ability to live it. But there is a direct correlation between the amount of information we gain and our level of frustration. It's frustrating to know about some-thing and not be able to live it. It's frustrating to know something is there and not be able to lay hold of it. It always seems elusive, like the carrot dangling in front of you that you keep chasing but can never grab.

In the things of the Spirit, no amount of know-about will give us the ability to *do*. Our heart is for God, though, so the more we know about, the greater our desire is to do it and the more we try to do it. But trying to live the Christian life through our own effort is like trying to put a cube into a spherical hole. It doesn't fit. The only One who can live the Chris-tian life is Christ. Only His life fits the hole. But we still try to force it to work ourselves, and that becomes very, very frustrating.

We are meant to be frustrated when we're trying to produce some-thing we're incapable of producing. It's the goodness of God to let us be frustrated. If God were to interrupt our frustration before we were completely frustrated, we would think, *I've learned how to do it. I'm not frustrated anymore.* But we wouldn't have learned anything. So He says, "Go right on with your program until you have exhausted the library of Christian literature on how to be spiritual. When you've exhausted all of that, when you've come to your end, you're ready to be taught by My Spirit. At that point, where else do you have to go?"

Without revelation knowledge from the Holy Spirit, we're not going to have an experiential understanding of the unseen and eternal reali-ties that are ours. Why does God make this so difficult? Don't ask me! It really isn't difficult, except that we are brought up living in the seen and temporal realm, and that makes the unseen and eternal realm seem difficult. We have to unlearn and be broken away from the first realm for the second to become reality to us.

This is God's plan. Our battles in the visible realm force us to finally ask the right question. Until we recognize that the right question doesn't focus on the externals of life, we're never going to experience the unseen and eternal. When we finally realize that the right question has to do with the life within us, then the Holy Spirit will come along with an answer. The only answers we get to flesh questions—those that focus on externals—are flesh answers. Those answers all have to do with more activity, more dedication, and more commitment. That's a flesh answer to a flesh question. It may even work for a little while. But it doesn't bring life.

The Spirit teaches us by bringing us to the place where we begin asking spirit questions instead of flesh questions. Spirit questions are questions from desperation. They arise when you reach the end of all your flesh questions. When we finally ask a spirit question, the Holy Spirit will give us an answer. It's interesting how quickly the answer comes once you ask the right question. Because the answer *always is* (present tense). All we have to do is catch up with the answer. The answer is a Person who lives in us.

This is why we have to fail. God couldn't be God and let us succeed in the flesh or we would never know Spirit life. We have the Spirit—we do contain the living God—but if we don't live out of Him, in our daily experience it's like we don't have Him in us at all. Our failures at living the Christian life press us into knowing Him as our life.

So how does the Spirit give us the answer? Paul explained in his first letter to the Corinthians. He began by talking about the hidden wisdom of God, a mystery the world does not understand:

> "Things which eye has not seen and ear has not heard,
> And which have not entered the heart of man,
> All that God has prepared for those who love Him"
> (1 Corinthians 2:9).

Paul isn't talking here about the sweet by-and-by. He's talking about now—what God has prepared for us in this life. He continues:

> For to us God revealed them through the Spirit; for the Spirit
> searches all things, even the depths of God (2:10).

The New King James Version translates it "the deep things of God."
We're all interested in the deep things of God. There's not a Christian
who doesn't want to go deeper into God. We may have become discouraged and given up on going deeper, but any believer wants to know God
intimately and wants the deep things of God revealed to him.

> For who among men knows the thoughts of a man except
> the spirit of the man which is in him? Even so the thoughts of
> God no one knows except the Spirit of God (2:11).

You could rephrase that last sentence to say this: no one knows God
but God. That puts us in a bad position, doesn't it? Because if God
doesn't tell us, we're never going to know.

So who is the real knower? The Spirit of God. He doesn't just know
about; He knows. *Knowing* is a Spirit word. It's an action of the Spirit
of God. It's also an action of the spirit of man. Our knower is our spirit.
But we are dependent upon the Spirit of God to bring knowing to us.
Because only He knows God and the deep things of God.

> Now we have received, not the spirit of the world, but the
> Spirit who is from God, so that we may know the things freely
> given to us by God (2:12).

In union with our spirit, the Spirit of God expresses His knowing to
us, and we know. By His revelation, we know the deep things of God.
And what are the deep things of God? Those things that God has freely
given to us. When the Spirit teaches us, we will see that everything in the
Christian life is a gift. When the fleshly mind tries to figure it out, it will
always be something that we earn. Know-about means we must earn it.
Know means we understand it's freely given.

When we live on know-about information, we live from separation—
not eternal separation, of course, but a sense of "God's up there; I'm
down here. I've got to try to make this life work, maybe even with His
help." We're busy trying to turn our life around. We want to make ourselves look like Christ. But when we know union, we know that His life

looks like us. When we know where Christ is, we know that Christ will look like us as we live our life. That's easy. Isn't it easy to be you?

That's a threat to people. Jesus knew that. He said, in essence, "I know who the Father is and I know where the Father is, so I know the Father looks like Me. He who has seen Me has seen the Father" (John 14:9). The religious leaders said, "That's blasphemy. You can't say that. You have to make your life look like God. Keep the law and your life will look like God's." One is separation. One is union. One is trying to earn. One is freely given. The Holy Spirit teaches us what God has freely given.

The only One who can make us one with the deep things of God is the Spirit of God. He is our one Teacher. Jesus said to the disciples, "But when He, the Spirit of truth, comes, He will guide you into all the truth" (John 16:13), and "the Helper, the Holy Spirit, whom the Father will send in My name, He will teach you all things, and bring to your remembrance all that I said to you" (John 14:26). We are dependent upon someone else to bring us truth. This is the role of the Holy Spirit within us as teacher.

My job when I used to travel around was to illustrate, to personalize, to underscore, to be a human instrument, but not to be the Teacher. Because if I teach you something, somebody else can un-teach you tomorrow. If I change your mind, somebody else can rechange your mind. But if the Spirit of God changes your mind, you're established in that truth.

For example, each of us as a believer has a spirit-knowing that our sins are forgiven. It's not an emotional knowing. It's not simply a fact knowing that's tied to a past event, whereby we remember the day we trusted Jesus Christ as our Savior. Spirit-knowing transcends that. We have an inner knowing that our sins are forgiven because the Holy Spirit has revealed it to us. In the same way, God wants us to know that we have been crucified with Christ and that it is no longer we who live, but Christ lives in us. That's the work of the Holy Spirit: to make a knower out of us, rather than a feeler or a thinker or a hoper.

Knowing is not feeling. It's not thinking. To someone who hasn't yet experienced the difference, knowing seems based on feelings and thoughts. But it isn't. In knowing, you and what you know are one. You become mixed, or united, with the thing you know.

The Holy Spirit teaches both by revelation and experience. The revelation can be instant and direct, without being transmitted by any formal teaching. We say, "Oh, I see." The Spirit then uses seen and temporal experiences to work that revelation into us. The revelation gets established in us through personal experience.

Some people have a hard time relating to that because they associate the word *teacher* with a schoolroom, where we just impart knowledge. But the Holy Spirit's teaching is experiential teaching. Of course, we do learn facts, but I'm talking about the process whereby we become one with what we are taught. We become one with the truth through experiential teaching.

This experiential knowing is indicated in the biblical words for "know." Both the Greek and Hebrew words for "know" that I'm referring to indicate experiential understanding of and oneness with. When "Adam knew his wife," it wasn't an intellectual thing. Adam experienced oneness with his wife. That's exactly what knowing is. There is no anxiety about those things that you know, because you become mixed with them. You and what you know are one.

On the natural level, I remember experiencing such knowing with high-school algebra. When it came to algebra, I didn't have a clue. I'd work those silly problems, and then I'd look up the answers in the back of the book. I'd get some answers right, but I didn't know how or why. None of it made sense. But one day the scales fell off my algebra eyes and it all made sense. I said, "Oh, I see! I see why you put this here and that there, change this sign, and so on." Then I could do it. I was relaxed about it. Until then I was striving and trying and working. Now I was at rest. I was one with algebra. Of course, we don't need the Spirit's revelation to do algebra. But it works the same in the spiritual realm.

When God gives you a flash of insight, that's it. You say, "Oh, I see!" and everything else, from then on, is just an elaboration on that flash. When you *know*, you are forever changed in that area. You'd have to make a conscious effort to go back on what the Holy Spirit showed you. That's why it's hard to sin in an area when the Holy Spirit truly shows you something. It's hard to go back on truth. Truth liberates.

I've always liked the word *awareness* more than the word *growth*. Because isn't that what really happens with us? Our *awareness* simply expands. We become more aware of Who our life is. We see more and more of Him. We're not seeing more and more *about* Him. We're seeing more and more *of* Him. He is the peace. He is the joy. He is the life. He is the love.

Until we see that, we are always saying to God, "Give me something. Gimme. Gimme. Gimme." But when that insight comes (and I'm not saying it has to be sudden, although it was with me), we say, "Oh, I see. I already have life. I already have Him."

When God gives your spirit a revelation, often your soul responds with, "That can't be." But your spirit is saying, "Yes, it is." Revelation doesn't take place in your brain. God reveals Himself in our spirit. He says, "Yes, the absolutes are true. When you begin to live in My reality, you'll begin to say, 'I am.' Until you live in My reality, you'll say, 'I am becoming' or 'I want to be' or 'I hope I am.'"

How many times have I said, "I'd like to be. I wish I were. Maybe someday." And God was on His throne saying, "You are! You are!" When we truly see that Christ is our life, time ceases to be a decisive factor for us. Everything is just now. We live in the present tense of God. He is not becoming. He is. You are not becoming. You are. You operate from "I am," not "I will become."

The unique thing about the Spirit of God as our teacher is that He has time to be an individual instructor to each one of us. He doesn't have a single lesson plan that fits everybody. He has tailor-made lesson plans based on our individual experiences, needs, and desires. So it's of little value for me to say to you, "This is the way He taught me." Because in all probability He never has taught you that way. He has taught you in His way for you, and it's just as real and valid as His way for me. The life experiences we have in the seen and temporal realm are the milieu out of which He does the teaching.

The encouraging news is that God is in control of this whole process: both when it will happen and to whom it will happen. He has chosen to reveal Himself, not to the chief muckety-mucks of the world system, but to us simple folk:

> At that time Jesus said, "I praise You, Father, Lord of heaven
> and earth, that You have hidden these things from the wise and

intelligent and have revealed them to infants. Yes, Father, for this way was well-pleasing in Your sight" (Matthew 11:25-26).

That seems a strange thing for God to do, but Paul understood it. He told the Corinthians that God has chosen the foolish things of the world to confound the wise. And look at you, Paul said. You're not much, by the world's standards. You're not the wisest in the world. You're not the cleverest. You're not looked upon as people of power, but God has chosen you.

Every revelation is according to God's good pleasure and His own timing. Timing is so important. You might get the itch before God wants to scratch. You think you're ready to stop the itch, but God may say, "You're not itching enough yet. If I were to meet you right now, it would be like harvesting something before its time. You wouldn't grow to full maturity." In His own way, in His own time, God reveals.

> "But when He, the Spirit of truth, comes, He will guide you into all the truth; for He will not speak on His own initiative, but whatever He hears, He will speak; and He will disclose to you what is to come. He will glorify Me, for He will take of Mine and will disclose it to you. All things that the Father has are Mine; therefore I said that He takes of Mine and will disclose it to you" (John 16:13-15).

The work of the Holy Spirit is to declare to us the Father and the Son within us. The Spirit makes no declaration about Himself. He attempts no glorification of Himself. He doesn't point to the fruit or the gifts. The Holy Spirit doesn't single Himself out because nothing originates with Him. The Spirit is the means by which the life of the Father and the Son comes forth. He wants us to know that we manifest the life of the Father and the Son. That is His revelation.

What can we do to cooperate with God's revelation to us? Agree with Him. Whether He has given your spirit a revelation on something or whether you simply read it in the Word but know that it's not yet an established part of your life, either way, just agree with Him. Knowing is always tied to believing. Sometimes we get a revelation and we just know. Sometimes we must choose to believe before we really know. We take something by faith, and then the knowing comes.

I finally had to say, "Lord, I'm tired of disagreeing with you. I'm tired of You saying through Your Spirit and the Word that certain things are true, and I'm saying back to you, 'They're not true.' The only thing this produces is inner dissatisfaction and unrest. I'm tired of this roller-coaster Christianity. Up and down. Hot and cold. Lord, I'm going to do something that is crazy for me. I'm going to agree with you. I'm going to believe three things, even though they don't look true in my life."

I said to God, "You say in Romans 8:1, 'There's no condemnation.' I've been saying there is condemnation. So now I agree with you. There is no condemnation for those who are in Christ Jesus. I am in Christ Jesus. There's no longer any condemnation for me. I won't take any more condemnation for anything that comes down the pike. And we'll see what happens."

There was a second one: no separation. I said, "Lord, all these years I've known nothing but separation. I've known some nearness to You, but nearness still has some space in it—varying degrees of separation. But You say there's no separation. I'll agree with you. There's never again any possibility of separation between me and You. If I'm really joined to You and You really express yourself through me, there's no separation. I agree with you."

Then the final one: God causes all things to work together for good. I said, "How can that be? I've spent my life saying things don't work together for good. But if You say they do, I'll agree with You. All things work together for good to me."

What was happening? I was only seeing God. Somehow He broke through my brain logjam and made His loving appeal to my spirit. And spirit wins out.

In the end, we always live out what we know. We can talk the talk and try to fool each other on Sundays, but when we get up Monday morning, we live out what we know. It's practically impossible to walk in what we don't know. Catch me off guard and you'll find out what I really know versus what I just talk about. My life will show it.

We have the privilege of knowing as God knows. The world doesn't know God's wisdom. It can't know it, because wisdom is not just the accumulation of facts. Using words that Paul wrote to the Ephesians, wisdom is the revelation of the knowledge of God. It's the revelation that God gives our spirit, plus the experience of the revelation. The experience of the revelation is what truly makes us knowers.

We receive a revelation, and then we get the experience of the revelation. The Holy Spirit works it into us, making us one with it. He does that through the noise and chaos of the seen and temporal realm: the world around us, our body, and our soul. These press us back into the knowing, into who we truly are, into "it is not me who lives, but Christ lives in me."

That's where the real life is. That's where the real knowing is. We are meant to know Him so that He can come forth from us, expressing Himself through us, as us. Then Jesus's words in John 4:14 are fulfilled. We are "a well of water springing up to eternal life."

12

The Single Eye

A number of years ago I was without medical insurance and I began having gall bladder problems. Eventually the doctors had to remove my gall bladder, and the operation cost me about $10,000. *Cash.*

I had been accumulating a little nest egg of savings, and it wiped that out. So I said to the Lord, "Okay, Lord. I know I'm cheap. And You know I'm cheap. So what was that all about? You didn't need to put me through that to tell either of us that I'm cheap. Why did we go through all of that?"

Soon thereafter, as I was driving home from church, He gave me an inner word. He said, "You know, you haven't had any difficulty with the fact that I am your source."

"That's right," I replied.

But He said, "You had a little bit of seen and temporal security. And your eye hadn't moved very much, but you were beginning to see that little nest egg and what you could add to that nest egg as your security."

So I went back and reminded myself: God put a certain amount of money in the bank for me. My immediate needs included three plane tickets, which I had already purchased. Then the operation came along, and I was able to pay for it and not owe anyone anything. And I didn't miss a single thing that I was scheduled to do. God told me: "Dan, I am not only your source; I am your security. That money isn't your security. I am your security."

I already knew that, but I hadn't ever really put it to the test. Looking for a God reason for what happened, I could see that as Mr. Cheap there wasn't anything that excited me more than adding to that little nest egg. But God had another purpose for that nest egg, to teach me this lesson: "I am your security."

I can tell that story and laugh about it, but only because of a choice I made. I could have chosen to see only external appearances, and I would still be bitter about having to spend the money. Or I could have chosen to see what God was doing in the situation. I chose the latter, and now I have laughter instead of bitterness. And I know as never before that He is my security.

Nothing happens in our life for which there isn't a God reason. If we don't want to see a God reason, we don't have to, and we will experience, or reap, only the external situation. In my case, I would have reaped more anger about being separated from my hard-earned cash.

Frankly, I would rather not have God's lessons for me be financial all the time, but that's my Achilles' heel, so God uses events in my life to work on that more than on something else.

The point is that God is our life now. The secret of the Christian life is learning to live out of the life of Another. Because that's true, we have to look at the things that happen to us in the natural realm from a supernatural point of view. Or, we could say, to look at seen and temporal events from an unseen and eternal perspective. We see what God is about in a situation.

God wouldn't have gotten my attention in that financial area without a specific incident for Him and me to focus on. There has to be a situation in our life to focus on, to spotlight, to cause us to stop in our tracks and look at something. Most of the things that cause us to stop and look have a disagreeable taste to us. We don't usually stop and examine the pleasant things that happen. The things that come against us, that hit us where we don't like to be hit, get our attention. I call this—seeing through our circumstances to God—the single eye. Jesus said,

> "The light of the body is the eye: if therefore thine eye be single,
> thy whole body shall be full of light. But if thine eye be evil,
> thy whole body shall be full of darkness. If therefore the light

that is in thee be darkness, how great is that darkness!" (Matthew 6:22-23 KJV).

Modern versions use "healthy," "good," or "clear" instead of the word "single." That is not incorrect, but those translations lose part of what the King James Version captures by using "single" to translate the Greek word. A single eye is healthy. A double eye would be evil. We get the same concept in James 1:8. A double-minded man is unstable. By contrast, a single mind is healthy. We need a single eye. Which means what?

It means we don't consider what we see and think—external appearances and our human evaluation of them—as absolutes in themselves. Granted, we have to initially see a situation or person based on appearances. That's how external information comes to us. But we take that information into us, and inside us is a union where God is all. In that spirit union, things have their source and their being in God regardless of how they appear.

The below-the-line realm is a realm of opposites. In the external world around us, things appear to be good or evil, pleasant or unpleasant, in use or misuse. Below the line is the realm of the Tree of the Knowledge of Good and Evil. But we are to look through both good and evil to God. For a moment we go past those opposites and we see only God. The double eye, which sees only below-the-line appearances, is unstable or evil. That's because if we see only below the line, we're not seeing total reality. If we see through to God, we see total reality. We see with a single eye.

With a single eye, we operate from just one inner Person, whose mind we have (1 Corinthians 2:16). In our spirit the only Person we see is God. We see through the unpleasant or the evil to God, just as we see through the pleasant or the good to God.

As long as we were living only below the line, with a spirit dead to God, we were going to see only that law of opposites: good and evil, sweet and sour, light and dark. But we are now born of God. When we are in God, and God only, God is all we see in life. Not Satan. God. We see God using Satan for His own ends. We move from seeing two to seeing one. Jesus said, "Blessed are the pure in heart, for they shall see God" (Matthew 5:8). *Pure* means unmixed. You see one. You are too pure to behold evil. You just see God.

In this seen and temporal realm we are privileged people. Through eyes of faith, we're given the privilege of seeing life as God sees it. We see that He is moving all things and events for the redemption and the filling of our lives and others' lives. There is not a single event in our life that God can't use either to bring us to Him or to cause His glory to shine through, causing someone else to see God in the way we handle a situation.

There is a great theological debate over who causes what—God or Satan. I try to stay out of that argument. I get lured into it every now and then because with a preacher's background, you almost can't help it. But you can get bogged down in who causes what. We could have a vote today on whether Satan caused something or God caused it, and it wouldn't do anybody any good; we'd just know the outcome of the vote.

It doesn't really matter who caused something. The real question is how am I going to take it into me? If I take it into me from God, then something positive is going to come out of it. If I don't take it into me from God, if I attribute the cause to Satan or any other person, then I'm going to get only a negative result out of it. I'm going to be pulled down even more into defeat or depression or wherever it is that I've been, until I can see God operating in that situation. I wasn't going to attribute my gall bladder attack to Satan. I could have, but I would have missed what God had for me through that circumstance.

I'm not saying there isn't a devil. I don't mean that sickness is not a result of the fall. Both are a reality. And it's not wrong if that's the level at which you see. But I believe God wants a group of people who can get beyond that. Yes, on one level we have to deal with the devil, but on another level we get beyond that. We begin to talk about our experiences the same way Jesus spoke of His approaching involvement with evil in the Garden of Gethsemane: "Shall I not drink the Father's cup?" The Father's cup.

In the seen and temporal realm, that cup was coming to Him from the evil one. But Jesus wouldn't take it that way, would He? The temptation was to take it that way. The temptation is always to see and experience life just like it looks and feels. But we won't get any victory there. For you who have told God that you want to go on with Him, that you want to know Him and Him only, the victory is to press on beyond the human situation. We move past what something looks like and feels like, to see by faith that God is involved in it. He has a purpose in it for us.

For those who have come to know this, one of the best things we can do is speak this word of truth to those who, in the midst of their circumstances, can't see God acting. We know He is acting in those circumstances, and we can be a word of encouragement to them. Often believers don't see that what they are going through is the way God is going to give them what they really want: Him.

We who know that this is His pattern can be a fleshly embodiment of support and an interpretive voice. We can stand as one with them, saying, "You know, this isn't lost time. It may have pain in it, but this isn't lost time. This is part of what God is doing to bring what you said you wanted into manifestation." It is amazing the drawing power of that word of hope.

When I listen to many teachers, I hear that message every now and then, but they usually don't mean it. Because to many of them, God isn't really working unless everything is on the upbeat. They'll talk about how God works through afflictions, but they don't really want God to work through their afflictions. What they really believe is that when everything is going great, then God is working. "He's in that," they'll say.

But we need to take the nasty, the ugly, the afflictions, the trials, and the tribulations, and identify them as part of God's domain. They, too, are His arena of operation. We're not debating now who caused something. We're talking about who is going to use it.

I love something my pastor once said: "What the Christian needs is 50/20 vision." He was referring to Genesis 50:20, where Joseph said of his brothers' actions against him: "You meant evil against me, but God meant it for good to bring about this present result." We need 50/20 vision. Most people just have the vision of, "It looks bad, it feels bad, so it *is* bad, and that's all it is." Then that's all they get. They get angry. They get bitter, because all they see is the external circumstance, which looks bad. But 50/20 vision says, "God means it for good."

There's no good news in just saying the devil did it. But there is good news in knowing God is going to work it together for good. God has another purpose in it. God is alive and well and at work, using the situation in your life.

The person who has come to know this is more at home in the unseen and eternal realm within than they are in the seen and temporal realm without. The seen and temporal realm says, "Yes, I can identify this as Satan; I can identify that as God. I can identify this as this and that as that." It's an external view.

We're not meant to leave that seen and temporal realm, because that's where the witness takes place. The life ministry occurs through you being yourself in that temporal realm. But what God wants is a whole host of sons and daughters who see as He sees and know as He knows. Spiritual adults know the Father's life. They know how the Father works. They know what Jeremiah knew, that whether it comes from seeming good or seeming bad, we choose to take it from God. All is of God.

Am I saying that God is the author of evil? By no means. But God in His sovereignty uses even evil to accomplish His purposes in us and in the world. Sometimes I use the expression, "He's in it, and He means it, but it's not His righteousness." An individual act may not be an expression of God's righteousness, but He's still in it, to use it for good.

We see this repeatedly in the Scriptures. Jeremiah records how the Jewish nation was taken into captivity in Babylon in 586 BC. God was in that, and God meant that, but the Jews weren't sent into captivity because they were expressing God's righteousness. If they had been, they wouldn't have been in captivity. Nevertheless, God was in that. God Himself said that Nebuchadnezzar is "My servant," and "Cyrus [king of Persia] is My anointed one." In the most negative example, God declared, "Pharaoh is Mine." Pharaoh was not expressing God's righteousness, but God was in that circumstance, and He meant Pharaoh's actions to occur. So God is in everything, and God means everything, but everything is not God.

Until you are willing to take the things of your life, push them on beyond Satan, and lay them at the Father's feet, you won't get peace. I'm not saying you might not get some resolution. God may deliver you from a bad circumstance. But I notice that when I hear people say, "God delivered me from this," or "God rescued so-and-so from that," the next one on their mind is the devil. Everything has to do with the devil.

Phooey on the devil. *God has already dealt with him!* And if the devil doesn't know it, you and I ought to know it. We watch God take the devil's tricks and lies and turn them around on him. They are the very horse manure out of which grows a beautiful plant. And we praise the Lord.

We all have what I call our lambs: some person, relationship, or event that God was willing to sacrifice for our growth. We don't know most spiritual truth without our lambs being sacrificed. Some wayward child, some ruined marriage, some lost job, these are your lambs. I don't excuse the sin involved in some of those things. But I'll tell you, if God's the only One in your life, and if He's the author of all your events, then you finally have to say, "Thank You, Jesus. Thank You, Jesus. Through that circumstance I came to know You, and knowing You is life. It hurt, but I know You."

God replies, "It hurt Me to know you too. It hurt Me to be able to get inside your skin and live there. You might have been abused, neglected, mocked, or treated unjustly, but I died to get inside your skin and be joined to you." What a God.

Sometimes our lamb can be the loss of a loved one. I took my wife Barbara's death right to the feet of the Father. I said the same thing I heard a precious woman say after I had preached the funeral for her 17-year-old son, who had died in an automobile wreck. As I preached my last word, she came to her feet and declared, "My boy lived every day he was supposed to live." Did knowing that immediately erase a mother's sorrow? Of course not. But she spoke the truth.

After Barbara died, I could say, "My Barbara lived every day she was supposed to live. She lived it gloriously. She lived it beautifully. She lived it simply. She lived it in faith. She was one of the purest souls I ever knew."

I don't care what your hurt is; you take it to the Father and you lay it right there. He will give you rest for your soul. I live in my spirit, and when I decide I want to grieve a little while, I'll drop down to my soul. I'll miss Barbara. I'll thank God for her. I'll wish she were here. I'll wish we could lie in bed and hug each other. I'll wish we could go out and eat together. When I have enjoyed that awhile, I return to my spirit. And I say, "God, all things are of you. I enjoyed that little party. My soul appreciated that. But I'm a spiritual being. And everything is all right."

Dry periods of our soul become oases for other people. God takes us through those dry periods, and then He uses them in other people's lives. We work on our testimony during our dry times. Later on, when we tell others about our dry times and how God brought us through them, people receive the life within us. That's where they plug in to us. They don't plug in to our self-righteousness. Nobody can relate to that. That puts people under, especially suffering people. Self-righteousness, "holiness" attained through self-effort, isn't the life. But when you can tell people about your time in the back side of the desert and about God's faithfulness, the true life flows out through you.

All of us will probably have more desert times. I don't like them. But when we experience such times, we can see they are going to serve the same purpose in our life that they have in the past.

People often tell me they can look back and see how God was in a past circumstance, but they're having trouble seeing Him in their current one. I respond, "Wait a minute. Isn't the same God who you just confessed brought you through all that garbage to get you here, isn't He the same One who's going to be around tomorrow and the next day? Yes! Well then, if He was in charge of the past, isn't He in charge of the present?"

They have to agree. Then they can say, "God, You were in that desert place, that hurt, that heartache, and You used all of it to bring me here. Surely I've got to expect that You are going to take me through this desert and future deserts. Because You are never going to cease preparing me to identify with others." Jesus endured suffering so that He could identify with us (Hebrews 2:9-18). God will do the same with us. We are for others. We need to know that God is in us for others.

When you begin to walk in oneness with God, you are no longer separating good and evil as it comes to you. Periodically you may be caught up in that, but the general tone of your life is that you no longer see that way. The experiences of your life are God experiences. The situations of your life are God situations. You see with a single eye. You see our sovereign Lover in all your life circumstances, no matter how they appear on the outside. And in the depths of your being you respond to His love, because you are one with Him.

13

The Rule of Grace

When my wife and I lived in South Carolina, she worked for a lady whose life began falling apart. This woman talked to a friend of mine, who led her to Christ. One day I took *The Key to Everything* by Norman Grubb over to her and said, "If the Lord leads you, read this booklet. If He leads you to read only one page, read one page. If there's anything you want to talk about, call me."

During the course of our conversation I told her, "You already have it all. You trusted Christ the other night, and there's not another thing God's going to be able to do for you. He hasn't got anything else to give you. He's given you Himself."

She started to ask, "If I decide to become religious—"

"Oh, please, don't become religious," I said. "For God's sake, don't become religious." I wanted to spare her from that. "Let's talk about life, not religion."

For most of us, living the Christian life is as difficult as finding Christ was. Often it's more difficult. Why? Now that we have Christ in us, shouldn't life go much easier?

The truth is that we ourselves make it difficult. We complicate it by trying to do what seems perfectly natural once we become a Christian. We try to keep God's law. But trying through our own effort to keep God's law prevents us from experiencing Christ's abundant life, because contrary to most popular teaching, it's the opposite of what God designed us to do.

Paul addressed the issue of the law in his letter to the Galatians. At the time he wrote to them, Paul had already been in Galatia once. He had personally preached the good news to the Galatians. Writing back, he told them that he was now "again in labor until Christ is formed in you" (4:19).

Previously, Paul had preached the message of Christ *for* them—His death on the cross for their sins. But if he had presented the message of Christ *in* them, it didn't take. The Galatians might have received his teaching about it, but they didn't get the revelation of it from the Holy Spirit. So Paul said, "I'm in the same birth pangs now as I was before, when I wanted to birth you into Christ. Now, I want to birth you into Christ in you." He wanted them to know Christ in them, the hope of glory (Colossians 1:27). Or, paraphrasing Galatians 2:20: "I live, but I don't live; Christ lives in me. And I want you to know that Christ lives in you."

Paul had a dedicated group of thorns in his flesh, however, called Judaizers. They would get hold of Paul's itinerary and show up after he had left a place, teaching that Jesus Christ alone is not enough. "You need the law," they proclaimed. "You must follow the law. There are some external things you have to do. You just can't say, 'Jesus Christ wipes the slate clean, and you can trust Jesus Christ to be your guide, and you can trust Jesus Christ to be your life.' You just can't go that far; that's too dangerous. You have to take this law along with Him."

Doesn't that sound logical? After all, it was God's own law, so we know it was good. Why then shouldn't the law—along with grace—be preached to the Galatians? Paul could have said, "Isn't this wonderful? I'm so glad these people have come along to keep you under the law."

But he didn't. What he did was tell the Galatians a story.

Years before, while Paul was in Antioch, Peter came up to visit from Jerusalem. Peter's home church in Jerusalem, of course, was 99.9 percent Jewish believers. Peter had had a revelation from God (Acts 10), and he knew that the gospel was for the Gentiles too. But he had never fully understood that the gospel couldn't blend with the law.

Remember, when Paul wrote about the law, he wasn't simply refer-ring to the Old Testament ceremonial and civil law. He was referring to the entire Old Testament law, particularly the moral law, summarized in the Ten Commandments. When he told the Romans (7:1-7) that they had died to the law, his example was Commandment Number Ten: "You shall not covet."

So in Antioch, Peter was fellowshipping with the Gentile believ-ers, but when Jewish believers arrived from Jerusalem, he withdrew and wouldn't fellowship with the Gentiles anymore. Paul confronted him publicly, because Peter was wrong:

> "We are Jews by nature and not sinners from among the Gen-tiles; nevertheless knowing that a man is not justified [made right with God] by the works of the Law but through faith in Christ Jesus, even we have believed in Christ Jesus, so that we may be justified by faith in Christ and not by the works of the Law; since by the works of the Law no flesh will be justi-fied" (Galatians 2:15-16).

Paul was saying, "Look, Peter, all of us have met Jesus. We used to be in the law, but we met Jesus, and life has come to us through Christ. Now what are we going to do? Lay something on these people that we were delivered from? Because that's what you're doing by insisting they keep the law."

Like Peter, the Galatians were putting themselves back under the law. Paul responded to them with equal indignation:

> You foolish Galatians, who has bewitched you…? [D]id you receive the Spirit by the works of the Law, or by hearing with faith? Are you so foolish? Having begun by the Spirit, are you now being perfected by the flesh? (3:1-3).

What was his point? These two ways of living, law and grace, are mor-tal enemies. Religion asserts, "No, they aren't mortal enemies. They can flow together, like the Missouri and Ohio rivers flow into the Mississippi, and they become the Mississippi."

Every place I've ever been in organized religion, I've found that belief.

But Paul was saying, "No, they never flow together. They've always been mortal enemies. They will always be mortal enemies. You can never marry the two. And you have to make a choice, Galatians. Are you going to live under law or under grace?"

Paul wasn't saying that if they stepped back into the law, they wouldn't be saved anymore. But he was telling them, "If you go back to the law, you're giving up the way of grace. And if you choose the law, here's the deal: you have to keep it all (see Galatians 3:10-14)."

They couldn't just pick out the laws they wanted to keep. That's what I used to do. I'd pick out those parts of Mosaic law, Sermon on the Mount law, Baptist law, my personal law, and whatever other law I thought I could keep at least some of the time. I didn't see that law and grace are mortal enemies. I didn't see that you can't live under both.

It made sense to me to be religious. It made sense to be an external Christian, trying to keep an external set of rules. I couldn't do anything else, because I had always been an external person. So were you. We all grew up as external people, defining ourselves in relation to other persons, things, and events that told us who we were. That's why as new Christians we were so prone to asking external questions: "What should I do?"

As I said to the woman in South Carolina, "Let's not talk about religion. Let's talk about life. Religion is law trying to become life. Life is life. They won't flow together."

There's no life in the law. The only thing the law tells you is what you ought to do but can't do. It will never relinquish its demand that you ought to do it, because it's a divine ought-to; after all, God gave it to Moses.

We'll keep ourselves under that divine ought-to, and the condemnation and death it ministers (2 Corinthians 3), until we learn to live from the Person who dwells within us. Because there's nothing in our flesh that wants to say, "I can't do it. I can't keep the law through my own effort." Everything in our flesh says, "I want to try to do it, and with God's help maybe I can do it." Like my friend Burt Rosenburg says, everything in that program is designed for futility, frustration, and failure. But they don't tell you that up front, do they? When you sign up, no one makes this announcement:

WE'VE GOT A WONDERFUL PROGRAM HERE, THE END RESULT OF WHICH WILL BE FUTILITY, FRUSTRATION, AND FAILURE! WHEN YOU HAVE COMPLETED THE COURSE, WE WILL GIVE YOU A DIPLOMA, SAYING:

"CONGRATULATIONS, YOU HAVE FAILED!"

I remember talking to a group and proclaiming, "We have succeeded! In what? In failing!" And everyone smiled. For we finally recognized that we had succeeded in what we were supposed to do, which was to fail. "Everyone is telling us that we failed in what we were supposed to succeed in. But the truth is we have succeeded in what we were supposed to fail in. Now, we can get on with it. We can get on with what is true life."

We usually quote Galatians 2:20 apart from its context. It immediately follows Paul's admonition to Peter concerning the law. When Paul said, "I have been crucified with Christ," he was referring to his death to the law. Paul was saying, "The old me died on the cross with Christ, and when I died, I died to trying to keep the law. Trying to keep the law is living according to the flesh, with me and my efforts as my point of reference. I died to myself as my point of reference. Now, Christ in me is my point of reference. He is living His life through me."

As believers, we no longer live under the law, looking to it to tell us what to do and not do, then trying our best to do it. Instead, we live on the faith principle, the inner life principle, of who really is our life— Christ. We trust that He directs us, opens or closes doors for us, and speaks directly to us, giving us a message or whatever is needed for the occasion. We trust that He is living through us. We may not feel it at any given moment, but we live by faith that He is our life.

In Galatians 3, Paul used the Old Testament itself to show that we live by grace through faith, not by the works of the law:

> Now the promises were spoken to Abraham and to his seed. He does not say, "And to seeds," as referring to many, but rather to one, "And to your seed," that is, Christ. What I am saying is this: the Law, which came four hundred and thirty years later, does not invalidate a covenant previously ratified by God, so as to nullify the promise. For if the inheritance is

based on law, it is no longer based on a promise; but God has granted it to Abraham by means of a promise (3:16-18).

God made a faith covenant with Abraham and with Christ, Abraham's seed. If God had said to Abraham, "And to your seeds," He would have included Abraham's entire lineage in establishing the covenant: all the patriarchs, Moses, Joshua, the prophets, and finally Christ. But God didn't say, "And to your seeds." He said, "And to your seed." The promises were made to Abraham and to Christ.

What point was Paul making? When we jump from Abraham to Christ, we jump 2000 years. And the most significant person we jump over is Moses. We jump Mosaic law. Paul goes straight from Abraham to Jesus. He leaps over the law. He doesn't try to fit it in there; he doesn't embrace it. On the contrary, he says that the inheritance can't be based on both the promise (grace) and the law. They are mutually exclusive. When Paul, the former Pharisee and champion of the law, had received God's revelation of the complete gospel, he jumped the law and landed right on Jesus.

Paul's antagonists taught, "Moses and Jesus." But Paul replied, "No way." Why did he say "no way"? For the same reason you and I could give from our own experience. There's no life in the law.

> For if a law had been given which was able to impart life, then righteousness would indeed have been based on law (Galatians 3:21).

There is no law that can impart life because law is always tied to self-effort. And self-effort can't produce life because only Jesus is the life. He has come to live His life in and through us. The law can only reveal our sin, condemn us for it, and show us our need for a Savior (Romans 3:20). Once it has done that, it has fulfilled its function. We are no longer under it (Galatians 3:24-25).

Isn't it amazing how the Bible gets interpreted these days, marrying law and grace? I used to do it. So did the Judaizers 2000 years ago. But Paul withstood their teaching. He knew that marrying law and grace would always be the death knell for the complete gospel: Christ in you, the hope of glory.

Few in Paul's day understood that you can't marry law and grace. Few today understand it. As a result, it can be a lonely life out there without the law. It isn't the easiest path, to walk in oneness with God, because no one ever sees Him. Yet you are believing that He lives in you and that your body is a temple of the living God, and you, like Jesus, say, "I just do what I hear from the Father." And you are going to live like that? There won't be many Christians around you affirming that kind of walk. But the Spirit will affirm it.

You have to know that you died to the law, because you never get away from the temptation to slip back into it. I never have, because there's something about the law that appeals to the flesh. When I'm sensing a little bit of a pull toward the law, I know that I would go back and swallow it all again if I didn't know that Christ really is my life.

Years ago I came to know a young man who was a fairly new believer and eagerly getting into the Word of God. I was talking to him about Christ living in us, and how we can live from Him within us. He replied, "No, you can't trust that! All you can trust is the Bible."

Well, I don't like getting into that debate because it sounds like you are against the Word. Praise the Lord that he was in the Word. I was just telling him, "You can trust the Spirit."

But he was saying, "No! No! No! It's got to be in the Bible!"

What I didn't know at the time was that less than two years before, he had been leading a seminar on motivation and mind control, and he would walk barefoot across a bed of hot coals without ever burning his feet. He had been following a spirit—a satanic spirit. So it made sense that he was leery of just trusting the Spirit. He wanted it all in black and white. But I didn't understand where he was coming from, and he didn't understand where I was coming from, so my final word to him was, "Well, I'll see you in ten years."

You have to go out and do it your way. If you have to follow the way of the law and experience futility, frustration, and failure, then you have to do that. Almost all of us do. This man loved God, but he wanted to reduce Christianity to a way to "do it," so I just had to let him find out for himself. God had him on the path He wanted him on, just as He has me on the path He wants me on, and we don't have to be on the same path at the same time.

The bottom line is this: law and grace won't flow together. They aren't compatible. One is sensible in appearance, but it is death. The other is absurd in appearance, but it is life.

I remember speaking to a group in Texas, to whom I had spoken many times. They had come to know experientially their union with Christ. I admitted to them, "I don't know any group I've seen in my all my years of traveling around that was more bound up in the law than you people. I never saw a more legalistic bunch of principle-keeping, dying-on-the-vine group in my whole life, and look at you now, living with Christ as your life. Isn't it wonderful? Have you ever stopped to thank God for the path He took you on? Because you see, there isn't anyone who's ever going to drive you back into the law again. You've jumped right over trying to keep the law, because you've done that aready."

No one was ever going to take Paul back to Moses, because he had done Moses. Someone could come along and claim, "You can marry Moses to Jesus," and Paul would reply, "No, you can't. I've already done the Moses thing."

That's why when someone comes to you and says, "Have you gone to the latest seminar on how to keep God's principles?" you can respond, "I've done it, man. I've done that one." And we've all done it. Like Abraham, we started out under grace; we received Jesus by faith. But we all went back under the law, trying to be pleasing to God through our own self-effort. Finally we jumped into who Jesus really is—the life. We won't be driven back into law again, because we've already done it, and we found it devoid of life.

Isn't that good, to have done it? It's time to thank God for the negatives. Thank God for whatever came between the time you trusted Jesus in simple faith and the time you began to trust Jesus as your life. Thank God for it, because that's what He uses to bring you to where you can say, with the same conviction and joy in your heart that Paul had, "I live, but no, I don't live; Christ is my life."

Once you have drunk from the wellspring of life, you can't be driven to any other place. There is a spring within you bubbling up, a spring of His life. You discover that it isn't out there somewhere. It isn't in the externals. It's inside you.

14

Who Does What?

Many people think the grace of God is like Him dropping a big, strong rope from heaven and giving you the privilege of trying to climb it. God does a little, then leaves the rest up to you. So you read *The Art of Rope Climbing* and *Seven Steps to Successful Rope Climbing*. You master those books and you get on the rope. But you climb about a tenth of the way up and you say, "This isn't going to work. I'm already exhausted."

So you start down.

I know, because I'm passing you on that same rope. I start up the rope and see you coming down. "What was your problem?" I ask. "Didn't you read that book on fifteen ways to climb the rope?"

Then I come down, exhausted, and here you are coming up again. "I'm going to make it this time!" you proclaim. Up and down, up and down, up and down.

That's what the Christian life is for most of us. It's all dealing with the false self, with below-the-line stuff, with trying to remold and remake the soul. The sad thing is that if we are successful in remaking it, the remade one isn't any better than the old one from God's point of view. It just knows how to cope better.

God's grace isn't a rope He dangles from heaven asking us to climb. We may understand that when it comes to our eternal salvation, but when it comes to living the Christian life, we turn around and ask, "Where is that rope?"

The Christian life is totally grace. God initiated it, God fulfills it, and God will complete it. He is the One who lives it in us.

Yet we may not know that it's totally grace. If we believe God has met 50 percent of His requirements by grace, then we think we have to fill up the other 50 percent by works. After all, 100 percent of His requirements have to be met, don't they? So if God has met only part of the requirement, it's up to us to meet the rest. Almost all of us have subtly been lured into that trap: "God saved me, He forgave my sins, but the rest is up to me."

A lady was telling me that John Wesley once said, "Earnestly pursue perfection."

I replied, "Good luck with that."

I earnestly pursued. Didn't you? I knew the forgiveness of my sins was by grace. But God had this demand, "be ye perfect, be ye holy." And though forgiveness was by grace, I was locked into doing the other part by works. I had to work to be holy. Even if 80 percent of it was by grace, I was going to have to do 20 percent by works.

The truth is this: it's *all* by grace. Not only is justification by grace, but sanctification is by grace. God does it all.

Hundreds of years before Christ came, God foretold that He would do it all. Through Ezekiel, He explained the New Covenant to the Jews:

> "Moreover, I will give you a new heart and put a new spirit within you; and I will remove the heart of stone from your flesh and give you a heart of flesh. I will put My Spirit within you and cause you to walk in My statutes, and you will be careful to observe My ordinances" (Ezekiel 36:26-27).

Who is the only one who can perform this heart transplant? God. Notice all of the "I wills" in this passage.

"I will give you a new heart."
"I will put a new spirit within you."
"I will remove the heart of stone."
"I will give you a heart of flesh."
"I will put My Spirit within you."
"I will cause you to walk in My statutes."

People often worry, "Can I keep the law? Can I live up to what God wants me to be?"

Of course, as Paul wrote, we have died to the law (Romans 7:4-6). We no longer have any relationship to it, nor do we look to it in an effort to fulfill it. But the law does reveal the character of God, and God's intent is to manifest His life through us. As He does that, He will Himself fulfill the law through us. Or, in other words, He will reflect His own character. So He says to us, "I will cause you to walk in them. After all, I'm the Lawgiver and the Lawkeeper, so I can cause you to walk in them."

Nothing of God has its point of origin with you. But everything of God will be manifested as you in your world. On the outside, it's going to look like you. But nothing is going to have its point of origin with you. The point of origin is God's "I will" in you.

Jeremiah was the first to record the New Covenant "I wills":

> "Behold, days are coming," declares the LORD, "when I will make a new covenant with the house of Israel and with the house of Judah...I will put My law within them and on their heart I will write it; and I will be their God, and they shall be My people. They will not teach again, each man his neighbor and each man his brother, saying, 'Know the LORD,' for they will all know Me, from the least of them to the greatest of them," declares the LORD, "for I will forgive their iniquity, and their sin I will remember no more" (31:31,33-34).

Aren't the "I wills" in Ezekiel and Jeremiah tremendous? God says, "I will do it." We are the benefactors of those "I wills." As those "I wills" are worked into us and become the reality of our lives, then we do walk in them. That's always been the desire of our hearts, to walk in the ways of the Lord.

As long as these things are just concepts to us, though, truths that seem separate from us, we try to make them happen ourselves. We are programmed to try to do it, but we don't know the inner life, so we are programmed for failure. We do have a new heart, and we want so desperately to do what God wants us to do, but we don't have the power to bring to pass what only God can do.

There isn't any way that we can make life succeed on any other basis than faith in God's "I wills." *He* will do it. That's the way it works. But it takes time for God to work His "I wills" into us and supplant our own "I wills."

Part of what God said He would do in Ezekiel is completed. He has given us a new heart. He has put a new spirit within us. He has removed our old heart and given us a new one, in which He has also placed His Spirit. That work, already finished, can't be touched. "He who is joined to the Lord is one spirit with Him" (1 Corinthians 6:17, NKJV). God can't do any more for us in the spirit realm than join His Spirit life to our human receiver spirit, and there be united with us in oneness.

The other part of God's work is ongoing. "I will cause you to walk in My statutes." That work of His proceeds in our soul and body. God is lining up our outer being with Himself. But until we see this unseen and eternal truth, we will try to line it up for Him. We will get hold of a new passage of Scripture, a new book, or a new concept, and say, "That's what I want to look like." And we will try to make it happen. I bought just about every how-to book ever written. I never did bother to ask if the authors could actually do it, but I quickly discovered I couldn't. God is the one who does it.

What role does the human being play in this divine encounter? Only one: to be willing. The only thing you can do is be willing and cooperate with the Person in you that can cause it to happen. God doesn't cause anything to happen internally that we don't want to happen. God never stomps on our will. He loves it, caresses it, enfolds it, and draws it to Himself, but He never overrides it.

It's a terrible blow to the ego to see that the only part you have to play in God's plan is willingness. A long time ago our foreparents bought a lie. In the Garden, they bought the lie of independent self and independent self-sufficiency. They believed that a real person was self-sufficient.

There are popular movements today built entirely on that premise. They're building up the self. You know what you get? More self. If you're successful, you get more vain. If you're not, you get self-condemnation. It's a dead end.

God does it all. Our part is to be willing. If we're willing and cooperate, "I will cause you to walk in My statutes and you will be careful to observe My ordinances." That's when it comes back to you—not as the point of origin but as the willing outward expresser of His life.

In Galatians 2:20, after saying, "I have been crucified with Christ; and it is no longer I who live, but Christ lives in me," Paul then talks of "the life which I now live in the flesh [the physical body]."

We do live, but Christ lives through us. "I will cause you to walk in them, but you will do it. I will cause it, but you will do it." That's the exciting part of this life, seeing God work out through us what He has worked into us. We see Him work out Whom He has worked in. And we are inwardly involved with all that He is doing.

God used the most disappointing chapter in my Christian life to begin to show me this. That episode became the necessary prerequisite for my greatest blessing. The Holy Spirit told me, "Look, you're trying to live a life you were never meant to live. But I can live the life in you, as you, that you're now trying to live on your own."

That's good news, isn't it? There is Someone who can live the life. He can live the life perfectly acceptable to the Father. Our primary role is to cooperate and be willing for Him to do it. He is willing, you are willing—that's the secret. He will live the life.

The Son has taken up His residence in us. His purpose is the same as it was during His earthly walk: to do the will of the Father. What the Holy Spirit does in us (not out through us in activity but in us as Teacher) is continually line us up with the true Person in us. That's why ongoing revelation is needed. The more understanding of His nature that He gives us, the more we fall in line with it, because that's the true desire of our new heart.

Previously, we were trying to produce this ourselves. Now, we're watching Him do it. We're being changed into His image from glory to glory by the Holy Spirit (2 Corinthians 3:18). More and more, without any kind of striving or effort, our whole will, indwelt by His Spirit's will, is just flowing with Him. We have always wanted to do His will. The Holy Spirit just brings that true desire to the surface, out from our spirit. Ultimately, we get to a place within where we don't know if something is our voice or His, because they become so one. So, like Jesus, we say, "My will is to do His will." Our will has been captured by God.

Sometimes people ask me: "If God does it, and He is living His life through me, what about the commands in the New Testament? We may have died to the Old Testament law, but aren't we supposed to try to keep God's commands?"

This is what I tell them. In 1 Corinthians 3:1, Paul talked about someone called "the soulical man" (often translated "carnal" or "fleshly"). The soulical believer is indwelt by Christ, but he doesn't know it. Or, if he does know about it, he doesn't know how to live out of it. He is living out of his soul. He operates as if life originates with him. He is living in Romans 7: "What I want to do, I don't, and vice versa." As a result, he is operating under the power of sin, which is energized by the law he puts himself under (1 Corinthians 15:56). He is still asking, "What do I do? How do I live it?" He thinks the life begins with him. He is a babe in Christ.

To the babes in Christ in Corinth (and I refer here not to chronological time since salvation but to spiritual maturity; a person saved for 50 years could still be a babe in Christ)—to these babes Paul said, "I gave you milk to drink, not solid food; for you were not yet able to receive it." After he gave them the good news that Christ died for them, Paul said, "I fed you with milk." What was the milk? I believe the milk was the dos and don'ts it was necessary to give them.

I found this to be true in my own ministry. I would travel around the country, always talking about Christ living in you, as you. Then I would get home and receive some letters. Often I would get a specific question: "What should I do about this situation?" or "What do you think about this decision?" So I would write back and give them an answer.

Paul often had a whole list of questions posed to him. When the people asked specific questions concerning real-life situations, he gave specific answers. Why? Because the people didn't yet know how to operate out of their true identity and their union with Christ, and they needed answers.

The Corinthians had questions about marriage. Paul answered them with some basic instructions. They had a problem with disputes going to court, and Paul responded. The believers in Thessalonica must have asked, "What about these guys? You told us Jesus was coming and they just quit working." Paul said, "If they don't work, they don't eat."

That's an immediate situation. These folks didn't have a Bible. They knew what to do only by asking someone who had passed through and taught them about Christ: Apollos, Aquila and Priscilla, Paul, or someone else. So they would send their questions, and Paul would send back his responses.

If you can't operate out of who you are yet, you want somebody to tell you what to do. We do that all the time. Even if we ourselves are living out of our union with Christ, we give people specific instruction that, because of the immediate situation, isn't really based on Christ in them. Instead, we provide a "to do" that meets an immediate need, all the while trusting that God will move them into a deeper experience of His life.

Many of Paul's letters were written to address specific problems. They were crisis letters, sent to address the need of the moment. But all of them may not reflect what Paul emphasized day by day. What we primarily have in Paul's letters are his answers to questions and heresies.

We don't have a record of what Paul taught daily when he stayed in Corinth for eighteen months or in Ephesus for three years. But we can get a pretty good idea of what he taught. To the Colossians, Paul wrote that he had been commissioned by God to preach

> the mystery which has been hidden from the past ages and generations, but has now been manifested to His saints… which is Christ in you, the hope of glory. We proclaim Him, admonishing every man and teaching every man with all wisdom, so that we may present every man complete in Christ (1:26-28).

The burning zeal of Paul's heart was to present every person complete in Christ. To accomplish that, He preached Christ in you, the hope of glory. He preached Christ living His life through them. He preached their union with Christ.

In the previous chapter we noted Paul's burden for the Galatians: "My children, with whom I am again in labor until Christ is formed in you" (4:19). Paul's focus for the churches was Christ in them. The other things were side issues. They were important issues, but they were momentary diversions from the main course. If we could have heard one of Paul's typical teaching sessions, I'm confident he would have been teaching "Christ in you."

Once someone begins living from the reality of Christ in them, which is the solid food of the gospel, they are weaned from the milk. They need the dos and don'ts less and less. They have learned to allow Christ to live His life through them. And the truth is this: Christ in us doesn't steal and isn't lazy and doesn't do all the other things Paul says not to do. But Christ in us doesn't need the dos and don'ts. He authored them. He lives them naturally through us as we learn to allow Him to.

So New Testament commands have their function, just as the Old Testament commands had their function as a tutor to lead us to Christ. But the commands are not the meat. They are the milk. The Holy Spirit's role is to bring us to a complete knowing of who Christ is in us and how Christ lives as us. When that has been done, He will fulfill the commands through us (Romans 8:4). But it will be His living, not our striving.

Knowing Christ in us—knowing that the gospel is 100 percent grace, that God does it all—frees us from the various labors that bogged us down for so many years. We thought these labors were our part, but we were wrong.

We can quit trying to be good. Our attempt just brings us despair, anyway, because we find out we can't do it. We are free from the facade of pretending that we can pull it off.

We can stop being religious. Jesus wasn't religious. He experienced life from the Father. The religionists wanted to kill Him, and did. We have as much religion today as they did back then. If we don't have a complete understanding of the grace of God, we will revert back to religion for our answer. We will use religious activity to say something about us, to make us acceptable to God, ourselves, and others. But when we see that Christ is formed in us, we're no longer religious. If God places us in a certain religious system (and He has with me), fine. But that doesn't mean we have to be religious. God has freed us from that.

We can stop trying to crucify ourselves. The old us is already dead. In the unseen and eternal realm, that's a done deal. But Christians have been trying to crucify themselves for the last 2000 years. As I always say, if you could crucify yourself, you'd crucify the wrong thing. We have something we want to get rid of for God's glory—a personality trait or some other displeasing thing. And He is shouting, "No, no, no, no!

What you've got is for My glory. That's what presses you into Me. You want to get rid of it so you'll look good for Me. I will crucify in you what's displeasing to Me, and I will magnify in you your weakness so I can be strong through it."

If God does it all, do we have any role to play? Absolutely. As I said earlier, our part is to be willing. Paul wrote, "work out your salvation with fear and trembling; for it is God who is at work in you, both to will and to work for His good pleasure" (Philippians 2:12-13). God is at work in us to choose and to perform His good pleasure. Our part is not to do it. Our part is to be willing. Our willingness is expressed as faith or trust. "I am willing for You to be living Your life through me this day, and I am trusting You to do it." Life for the believer operates by faith, not by self-effort.

Sometimes people hear the full message of God's grace and respond, "But doesn't God call us to be obedient?" Yes, there is an obedience God calls us to. Paul called it the obedience of faith (Romans 1:5). You obey by believing. You became a believer through the obedience of faith. You believed that Christ died for your sins. You having died with Christ works the same way as Christ having died for you. In both cases, you have to put faith in an unseen and eternal truth before you begin to see it operate in your life.

The work of faith is not to try to do the dying. The work of faith is to recall that the old you did die and to live out of that fact. We remember and count on the revelation fact. If it's not a revelation fact, then you are striving to get hold of something you think you don't have. There's no guilt in that, because what else can you do than strive for something if you don't know you have it? But the truth is we already have it. In the unseen and eternal, the old us is already dead. The faith life on our part occurs when the circumstances arrive that say, "The old you isn't dead," and we reply, "Yes, he is." But we aren't trying to accomplish it, because how can we accomplish something that's already accomplished?

Paul had another word for this process in Romans. He called it reckoning. *Reckon* is a banking word. It means you can count on money in the bank when you go shopping. You can write checks because there's money in the bank. Reckoning doesn't put money in the bank. But counting on the fact that there is money in the bank will free you to write checks. After explaining that we have died and been raised with Christ, Paul said, "Even so consider [reckon] yourselves to be dead to sin, but alive to God in Christ Jesus" (Romans 6:11).

You are dead to sin. You are alive to God. Reckoning doesn't make it so. It is already so. But reckoning allows you to live out of the fact that it is so.

God says you are a brand-new creature. The old one died. You don't look dead, you don't feel dead, you don't always act dead, but are you going to agree with God or are you going to debate Him? You may debate Him, but you're going to lose the debate. It's not worth it. So in faith you agree with God: "I read that, and it sounds too good to be true, but I'm going to believe that. I'm going to set my face to that."

The truth is that when we first trusted Christ, we were made perfect (Hebrews 10:14). We were complete in Him (Colossians 2:10). But who knew it at that point? So we thrashed about below the line in all of our soul activity, trusting in appearances instead of God's truth. All we ever do is catch up with the truth. Through our trust in God's revelation, His truth becomes our experience.

If we never get to the point where we appropriate truth, we are caught in a flesh trap forever. God has designed life so that our will, which He is at work in, has a role to play. We have to choose to trust Christ in us.

God spoke to me one time about that in Denver. I was playing golf, and I was my usual incorrigible self. I was so disgusted with the quality of my play that I had resorted to using only one club. I drove with it. I hit from the rough with it. I knocked balls out of sand traps with it. I putted with it. I didn't speak to the woman I was sharing a cart with. My wife was ahead of us with another lady. I was just going through the motions, waiting to get the miserable experience over with. On the back nine, my partner looked at me and said, "Jesus sure acts like a baby in you." And I thought, *That's God.*

I am in charge of whether Jesus looks like a baby in me or not. We must act on what God says, because we are involved with Him in this. We must choose to trust Him. Ours is a covenant relationship, and faith is the operating principle. "I speak to you, and you respond to Me. You trust Me." We are not lost in this union relationship. We are a vital part of it. God invites us to be cooperators with Him.

Humanity was created in the beginning with the capacity to receive the Tree of Life (which is Christ) and then to be an expresser of that life. That was God's original intent. But God purposely created us with the possibility of choice, and we reap the results of our choice. We never escape that—then or now. In God's love, He lets us choose. He says, "If you want to go the way of the world, go. If that's where your love and affection is, you go. But you'll reap what you have chosen."

Does that mean all is not of grace? No. God does do it all. Only He can live the life. And only He can work in us, enabling us to be willing cooperators with Him. But He has left us a role. Our role is availability. We are available to the Lord to live His life through us. What Mary said to the angel Gabriel applies to every believer: "Behold, the bond-slave of the Lord; may it be done to me according to your word" (Luke 1:38). That's availability. Mary was willing. God was the one who did it.

Our availability releases God's ability. So we trust the Lord to do it through us.

"Lord, You want to love this person through me. I'm not feeling loving toward them. You do the loving through me. I make myself available for that."

"Lord, I'm feeling bitter toward this person. I choose to allow You to be forgiving through me."

"Lord, I don't feel like serving this person. But You do. You go the second mile through me."

Apart from Christ, humanity isn't going to do that. But that's the nature of the One who is in you. You can say to Him, "You do it. I am willing for You to do the willing. You take over here."

In the unseen and eternal realm of God, things that don't seem to be finished already are; things that don't seem to be complete already are; someone who doesn't yet appear to be mature or full-grown already is. Until we get revelation knowledge of that, we are going to try to accomplish these things by ourselves. Our point of reference is still going to be ourselves. We will keep trying to make it happen until we get a complete picture of the grace of God. Then we will see that it's already done. He does it. He does it all.

15

God's Process of Growth

God's goal is to take us from external to internal, from looking for life in this world, in the body, or in the soul to experiencing true life in the union of our spirit with God's Spirit.

He can take many routes to get us there. The route He took me was from Jesus as Savior to Jesus as Filler to Jesus as Life. But that isn't everybody's route. Some folks add in different stops along the way. God isn't limited to any specific process. He will do whatever it takes to present us full grown, mature, and whole in Christ below the line. We already are that way above the line. He wants our everyday life to express what is already true about us.

In this chapter I want to present three different ways that we can look at Christian growth, or the process God uses to mature us. I present three because there is no one way to look at the maturation process. Growth is a dynamic thing that can't be put into a neat little box or formula. Why would we expect anything else? The God of all creation is the One at work in us. We have only to look at a colorful sunset to see that He delights in diversity. So also He delights in bringing us to maturity in diverse ways.

The three processes I describe here are like viewing a gem from various angles. They are simply different perspectives, all describing essentially the same thing. By presenting three, I pray the Lord will take at least one and touch your heart, using it to encourage you and draw you deeper into Him.

The first illustration of God's process of growth comes from 1 John 2:12-14, where the apostle described stages of growth that believers go through. He didn't say whether all believers go through these exact stages, but I believe they are descriptive of God's path for most of us. He said,

> I am writing to you, little children, because your sins have been forgiven you for His name's sake. I am writing to you, fathers, because you know Him who has been from the beginning. I am writing to you, young men, because you have overcome the evil one. I have written to you, children, because you know the Father. I have written to you, fathers, because you know Him who has been from the beginning. I have written to you, young men, because you are strong, and the word of God abides in you, and you have overcome the evil one (1 John 2:12-14).

Under the roof of the house of God, the Body of Christ, John sees three kinds of believers. None of these people are called little children, young men, or fathers because of their chronological age. He isn't talking about the nursery, the youth department, and the adult Sunday school. All three designations are based on people's level of inner knowing.

The little children know two things: (1) their sins have been forgiven, and (2) they have a relationship with the Father. That's all they know. They may *know about* a lot of things, but they *know* these two things. The vast majority of Christians, I believe, are in this stage.

The middle group, the young men, know three things: (1) they know they are strong, (2) they know the word of God abides in them, and (3) they know they have overcome the evil one. They still know what they knew as little children—that their sins are forgiven and that they have a relationship with the Father—but now they know these other things as well. They have moved beyond the little children stage.

But notice where the young men's emphasis remains. The emphasis is on them. *They* are strong. *They* have overcome the evil one. The word of God abides in *them*. Their point of reference is still largely themselves: "Look what has happened to me; look at what I have done."

What excites the young men most is power. "You will receive power when the Holy Spirit has come upon you" (Acts 1:8). Isn't that like young people? They love power. They love strength. They love excitement. They love adventure. But the entire world still centers on them. They are still their own point of reference.

There's nothing wrong with this stage. Each group is operating from all the revelation it has at that moment. The young men have had much more revelation from God about what it means to be a Christian. They have probably moved into the position of knowing Christ in them, to help them (but not to live through them, as them).

But there is a third group: fathers. John twice says one thing about them: they know Him who is from the beginning. The Bible's first four words are "in the beginning God." Fathers know God. They don't just know power; they know Person. Fathers have entered into Person. They recognize that they are in union, not with one aspect of God—power—but with the personhood of God. They know Him who has been, is, and ever will be. They know the I AM. When you come to the father stage, it's no longer what you know. It's Whom you know.

It's easy for us to be suspicious or fearful of what we don't yet know or haven't yet experienced. The little children can be suspicious of the young men and the fathers, because they haven't experienced what the latter two have. Likewise, the young men may be suspicious of the fathers, because they aren't there yet, and they wonder why the fathers aren't doing all the things they're doing.

When you become a father, you're settled in. You're calm. The young men are still running around wanting to make war and do battle. In comparison, you as a father look pale because you're not putting on your armor, taking up arms, and slaying dragons all over the place. But there's no reason for you to be upset with the young men (or the little children). You've been a young man. You know that's a spiritual stage that's right and appropriate. So you can say, "Praise the Lord. I've been there too."

There's no reason for fathers to be anything but understanding, sympathetic, and compassionate toward those who are at earlier stages. You've already been there, and the Holy Spirit has taught you that every one of those steps was important and necessary. You are living out of the realm of spirit at all times, and you are spiritually discerning. "He who is spiritual appraises all things" (1 Corinthians 2:15). You can see what's going on because you are seeing from an inner eye that has been enlightened.

God invites us all to the father stage. It is a stage of living by faith, not sight. It's a stage of "the fellowship of His sufferings," where Christ's death operates in our soul so that life can come out for others (2 Corinthians 4:12). But it is a stage of *rest*. We experience our union with the One who is without beginning or end. He is love, and He moves out through us in love to embrace this world and be life to others.

The second illustration of the process of growth is what I call recapturing the soul as manifestor of God. St. John of the Cross spoke about the human being getting to a place where his or her life is like a windowpane. God in us, behind that windowpane, shines through without any distortion. But most of our lives are not clear windowpanes.

Of course, we will never expect them to be perfectly clear, but we are talking about growth here. St. John of the Cross's point was that if we are trying to *do* for God, then our fingerprints are all over that windowpane. If a windowpane has fingerprints all over it, you can still see a person through it, but the image is distorted. I think the desire to have a clear windowpane is proportional to the intensity of our love for God. But our flesh, in the negative sense, often gets in the way.

My life notebook is full of flesh. One day my wife and I both needed to write a check at the same time, and she went over and sat down at my desk. *My* desk.

I said, "What are you doing at my desk? All your stuff is over there across the room. Besides, you gave me this desk and said it was mine."

She did. She gave me that desk for Christmas and said it was mine. And there she was, sitting down at it, writing a check at the very moment I needed to be there. Momentarily she got up and left for work. She had hardly gotten out the door before God said to me, "You're being a jerk. What do you mean 'my desk'? Is that your desk?"

When she came home for lunch I said, "Barbara, I'm sorry. I don't have a desk."

"I've been wondering all morning why you acted like that," she replied.

"It was because of the possessive pronoun *my*—'my desk.'"

To me, my reaction had been a fingerprint on the windowpane. I don't mean that God didn't use it. He used it on me within minutes.

John the Baptist said it: "He must increase, but I must decrease." That increase takes place in the soul. The intensity of the battle isn't in the spirit. Calmness and tranquility and serenity reign in the spirit. The turmoil is in recapturing the soul, where God moves out to retake the territory that was stolen from Him—territory He originally made so that He could manifest Himself by means of us. But we have a long history of being captured goods.

I remember years ago reading a story in *Reader's Digest* of an American military man who helped liberate a prisoner of war camp in Germany at the end of World War II. In the blink of an eye the camp's captives were now the free people, and the formerly free people, the German soldiers, were now the captives. But neither group knew how to act. The men who had been behind the barbed wire for so long were told they were free, and they just stood there.

That's the way my soul is many times. It has been freed from captivity. It's the vehicle of the Holy Spirit. It's the vehicle by which Almighty God wants to manifest Himself. But some old grave clothes are still hanging on it. Old habits and patterns that were ingrained in me for years and years still emerge from time to time. Some people are able to say, "Well, that's okay. What can you do about it? If that happens, it happens." But it breaks my heart.

I was speaking to a group I had spoken to many times before and who had, by and large, experienced their union with Christ. I said:

> We who have come to know our union with Christ have had difficulty with the word *responsibility*. I was studying that word and you know where it comes from? It comes from the same word as *respond*. You can look God in the face and say, "I don't believe in responsibility," but I'll tell you a secret: He'll never capture one inch of your soul with that attitude. Because what you're really saying to Him is, "I'm going to be like I am. I don't care. I'm going to be like this. I dare You to change me."

We talk about knowing God. Knowing God means being passionate about letting God take us in love. The process of God tenderizing our soul may be painful at times, but it is us responding to the love of God and loving Him in return.

God calls us to be responders to Him. The ultimate thing a human does is hear God and obey. You don't have to answer to anybody else for what your obedience looks like. It will probably look like foolishness. But in your heart of hearts, you know that you were obedient. And you have allowed Him to take your soul in love.

I wouldn't work on my soul the way God usually does. I told you earlier about the $10,000 that I had to spend on a gall bladder operation. Not long after that, Barbara wanted to trade our car in for another one. To keep peace in the family, I traded it in. I didn't even like the new car. In addition, for the first time in my life I had a car payment. Previously, I had always paid cash for cars. So I had this big monthly payment at a horrendous interest rate.

I went to speak at a conference and was mulling over our new car purchase. I always know I'm in trouble when I begin to think, *If I could die, I could get out of this.* If your soul is prone to depression, you know that's what you do. Suddenly my life, which I had wanted to be moving toward simplification, had become complicated again. I had a car payment at the same time that my ministry was diminishing. I said, "God, don't you have anybody else you can work on? Why do I get all of this attention?"

When God works on the soul, He doesn't give you a list of choices to pick from. God has already ordained the way He is going to work on you, and it's called life—and sometimes we just don't like it. We say, "Just give me a book to read about it. Give me a cerebral way to understand what You want to do, and maybe I can ease into this lesson without all this trauma."

But it doesn't work that way. God uses the storms in the soul to force us back into the truth. We go back into spirit and we thank Him for it. In that inner place, where His Spirit is joined to our spirit, He is at rest in us, and we are at rest in Him.

God takes the world, which lies in the hands of the evil one and is a system currently kidnapped into the duality of good and evil, and uses that very world system to purify us. But if we don't know that, we're not likely to have more purification. We will only have more hostility toward God, because we won't see beyond the human situation to the divine purpose in it.

If something has a divine purpose behind it, we can accept it, by the grace of God. Previously, we complained, "How can there be any divine purpose in this? I'm just getting crushed down." So we suffered a permanent "poor me" syndrome. That's where the world strikes us first, isn't it? It hits us on the external us. It strikes us in the senses, which then move back into our feelings. That's God's way too.

When our feelings were the deepest thing we knew about ourselves, we thought that was the deepest thing there was. So we were in constant pain and turmoil. But now we can be in the midst of difficult situations and still speak truth. As I said earlier, it's like being in the middle of a hurricane. The eye of the storm is calm. We return to our place of safety.

There's a hymn that starts with the words, "There is a place of quiet rest near to the heart of God." I change that to "in the heart of God." We are in Him. He is in us. As we rest there, God continues to peel the onion called our soul, aligning our outer person more and more with His inner person, wiping the smudges off the windowpane of our soul, recapturing our soul as the manifestor of Him.

When I went around the country giving talks, I used live props for my third illustration of God's process of growth. I would have four people come stand at the front. One would be God (a big role, I know). One would be the human spirit, side by side with God, indicating the permanent union between our spirit and God's Spirit, the two functioning as one unit. One would be the soul, standing in front of the human spirit. The last would be the body, standing in front, indicating the permanent union between our spirit and God's Spirit, the two functioning as one unit.

All faced the audience. God designed the body exactly that way, to face outward, to receive its input from the external world, through the senses, and to transmit that information back to the soul.

God designed the soul to face the spirit, to receive its primary input and direction and life from the spirit. We are meant to hear God speak. But mankind's fall changed that. Because of the fall, the soul is also turned outward, toward the body. Satan, through the senses, lured the soul to turn from its original purpose, from being an agent of the spirit, to instead being an agent of the body. That's why the Bible talks about fleshly sins—bodily sins.

The soul of the unregenerate person gets all of its information externally. It has been completely wooed away from what it was supposed to be, turned toward the spirit/Spirit. It is turned outward, and it is carrying out the dictates of its captor, Satan. As believers, though, we are regenerated at salvation and no part of us, including the soul and body, is truly captive to Satan.

However, until a person knows who he is and is living out of his union with Christ, the soul for the most part remains as it was. It remains turned outward, receiving its input and direction and trying to receive its life from the pleasures of the body and world. But it wasn't created to be that way.

This is Christian growth: the Father/Son/Spirit wooing our soul back from its fascination with the outer (the body and the world) to a fascination with the inner (the Spirit/spirit in union). Growing in Christ doesn't mean increasingly getting our act together, but being wooed back. The entirety of our Christian life is the process of our soul turning back to our spirit.

God wants to woo us back in every area that our soul is turned outward. Wherever we aren't wooed back, we are vulnerable to the call of the outer—our body and its appetites, the world, or Satan.

Let's say you're not yet wooed back in the area of material possessions. You are greedy or covetous. That's the heart of all temptation, to satisfy ourselves our own way. But you begin to get a deeper taste of the Spirit. And slowly you let the Spirit/spirit woo you back in this area of greed and covetousness to where you can say, "I recognize the answer to my greed. Christ is totally sufficient. I don't have to satisfy my needs that way. Christ is meeting my needs this very moment." So you are wooed back in that area.

Maybe you are bitter toward a family member. The Spirit woos you back in the area of bitterness. You are finally able to say, "I don't need to be bitter. The Spirit of God is my sufficiency."

So you are wooed back to the point where, for the most part, that temptation doesn't bother you anymore. That's not to say you will never be tempted, but you have learned that Christ is your sufficiency in that area. The lie behind that temptation isn't your life. You know that Christ in you is your life.

Do you see what life is all about? God means to turn the whole soul slowly back to Him, to the union of His Spirit and our spirit. He isn't concerned about instant below-the-line perfection. He wants steady progress in our inner knowing. Christian growth isn't us striving. It's us letting the Spirit woo us back, woo our soul back, so that we are preoccupied with Him, and we are expressions of Him to the world.

Part Five

Living in Union

16

Will Not Hunger

Jesus said something in the Gospel of John that we all know but few of us have really thought through:

> "I am the bread of life; he who comes to Me will not hunger, and he who believes in Me will never thirst" (John 6:35).

Have we come to Him?

Jesus simply says, "He who comes to Me…" There are no extra conditions or comparisons. If we are believers, we *have* come to Him.

What else does He say? "He who believes in Me…"

Haven't we believed in Him? Yes, we have believed. There's no adverb there to indicate some kind of supercharged belief. He just says, "He who believes…"

What does Jesus say about us who have come to Him and believed? They "will not hunger…will never thirst."

One day the Holy Spirit lifted a word off that page of my Bible in bright neon lights: *never. NEVER!*

Never is a strong word. I try to avoid it. Sometimes when I'm giving a talk I find myself using *never*, only to back up and say, "That's too strong a word." With *never*, there's no outlet. There's no loophole in *never*. But Jesus said, "He who comes to Me will not hunger, and he who believes in Me will never thirst."

Below the line, we live from soulish hunger. We say, "I'm so hungry.

I'm so thirsty. I need. I'm just hanging on by my fingernails. I haven't cut them in weeks so I can keep hanging on." We're speaking from a hunger, from a sense of separation, a sense of nonfulfillment, a sense of lack.

But Jesus says that we will never hunger or thirst.

As John does so often in his Gospel, he's giving us above-the-line spiritual truth in John 6. We see this later in the chapter when Jesus said, "It is the Spirit who gives life; the flesh profits nothing; the words that I have spoken to you are spirit and are life" (6:63).

Jesus isn't addressing our below-the-line soulish hunger. The context in which we never hunger and never thirst is the realm of spirit. He is saying that if I know whom I am in union with—God the Father, God the Son, and God the Holy Spirit—if I know and live from that, there's no such thing as hunger or thirst. You're never hungry. You're never thirsty.

Do you get the implication? Jesus is our total spirit sufficiency. We need to know that if we're going to be light to others. We need to know that our lightbulb isn't going to run out of juice, or else we will constantly be worried about satisfying our own hunger. For the person who knows he is in Christ and Christ is in him, there's no occasion for a sense of lack. Jesus says, "I am your total sufficiency."

We come to know that only by revelation.

Jesus made similar statements in surrounding chapters of John. To the woman at the well He said,

> "Everyone who drinks of this [physical] water will thirst again; but whoever drinks of the water that I will give him shall never thirst; but the water that I will give him will become in him a well of water springing up to eternal life" (John 4:13-14).

Have we drunk? Yes, we have permanently drunk. Will we ever thirst? No. Are we ever going to run out of that water? It's a well of water springing up and bubbling over. It never runs dry.

At the Jewish feast in Jerusalem Jesus cried out,

> "If anyone is thirsty, let him come to Me and drink. He who believes in Me, as the Scripture said, 'From his innermost being will flow rivers of living water'" (John 7:37-38).

Again, have we believed? So what is going to flow from our innermost being? Rivers of living water, which according to the next verse refers to the Holy Spirit. The Holy Spirit needs to show us that by revelation. Too many of us have settled for a trickle when God has more for us.

Rivers of living water flow out of you. If the river comes out of you, which direction does it flow? Away from you. So you can't run down to the river and drink your own spiritual water. We have to know that Christ Himself is this very moment filling us. We can rest, knowing that we're not hungry or thirsty. Jesus says, "I am your total sufficiency."

However, someone may ask, what about Matthew 6:33? "Seek first His kingdom and His righteousness, and all these things will be added to you." The "these things" are below-the-line items: food and clothing. Jesus promised that if we seek first the kingdom of God, we will have these things supplied. Another verse tells us to seek: "So I say to you, ask, and it will be given to you; seek, and you will find; knock, and it will be opened to you" (Luke 11:9).

I thought I was doomed to be a seeker forever. I thought I'd never find what I was looking for. I was taught, "You're saved, so now you just keep on seeking the kingdom, keep on seeking, keep on seeking..." Perpetual labor and striving. But I discovered that through union with Christ, I'm no longer a seeker. I'm a finder.

Jesus said the kingdom of God is where? In us. Every kingdom has a king. And the King lives in us. The basic definition of the kingdom of God is the rule and reign of God. Well, that's taken place in our heart, hasn't it? So we're no longer seeking the kingdom. We're finders. Whatever the kingdom of God may look like in the future in the external, it has already begun internally for us.

What does that do for us? It frees us. We no longer need to be preoccupied or anxious about ourselves and our spiritual state. I used to run around in circles where it was spiritual to talk about "needing a filling." Or "getting into the Word so that God can fill you." Those things are important, but once you know you're filled, then you can't be filled any more than that. If you know Christ is your life, then you're not out trying to get life. He has already filled your spirit hunger.

But that doesn't mean that on a given day our soul can't feel hungry and thirsty. We still have this outer person, our soul that's subject to playing that old tape about us feeling needy. It plays again and again. Our privilege is to remind ourselves of the truth: "I am your total sufficiency."

There's nothing spiritual about saying you're seeking more of Jesus. Because He can't give you any more. He can give you more awareness about Whom you already have, but He can't give you any more of Him. You've got Him, and He's got you. The needs that preoccupy us so much of the time, that keep us focused on ourselves, have already been met in Christ.

David's life illustrates the problem we get into by believing we have needs that God is not meeting this moment. The Bible says that David was a man after God's own heart. But he was also a man with all power in Israel. It's difficult to handle power because everything is at your disposal. So he abused his power, committed adultery with Bathsheba, and then murdered to cover it up.

Why did David get in such trouble? He was listening to a lie. He thought he had a need that God wasn't meeting. Satan plays that same trick on you and me. His secret is to raise within us a question about God's sufficiency for our lives. As my friend Bill Hodge says, the devil's favorite word is *if*.

"*If* God is your source, why is your husband without a job?"

"*If* God is your life, why did your wife have to die?"

"*If* God is your sufficiency, why is your child strung out and rebellious?"

We think, *Well, I don't know. Maybe I need something else. Maybe I need…* Satan begins to provide the noise in our life, the external distractions, to supply that need he's creating within us. It's a lie. We need to live in the truth, not a lie.

I sat beside Barbara and watched her life go. And I rejoiced. I hurt, but I rejoiced. I rejoice now for the forty plus years we had together. I rejoice that she's gone to be with the Lord. I rejoice that she's not in pain. Even though there are times when I could say, "I wish you were here," my sufficiency for these days is my precious God. He has become my wife. I don't deny the sadness, but my life is not in the sadness.

People are constantly wrestling with the flesh instead of getting on their knees and thanking God, "It took You leading me down this path for me to know You." It took someone else, maybe that child, that husband, that wife, to be the one God used to bring us to the place where we could experience His life.

Jesus Himself is our sufficiency. Perhaps the Scriptures never present that so clearly as in John 11 when Lazarus, the brother of Mary and Martha, fell ill. After hearing the news, Jesus purposely delayed going to Bethany so that Lazarus would already be dead when He arrived. When He and the disciples finally arrived at the home of Mary and Martha, a wake was already in progress.

Jesus was encountered by Martha first, who spoke in terms of past and future. The past was, "Lord, if You had been here, my brother would not have died." The future was, "I know that he will rise again in the resurrection on the last day." But there was no sense of the present tense with her.

It's ironic that she made those remarks about the past and the future to the One who is the I AM, who knows no past or future and lives only in the present. "I who stand before you am the resurrection and the life. That which you await in the future tense, in Me is reality now."

Martha brought Mary to Jesus. She also was past tense: "Lord, if You had been here, my brother would not have died." Although we know from elsewhere that the sisters differed considerably, in this time of crisis their comprehension of the presentness of Jesus Christ was similarly lacking. Isn't that true of all of us? There are times in which the immediate awareness of God's presentness is not as much reality to us as the past or the future. By bringing Lazarus back from the dead, Jesus demonstrated for Mary and Martha His sufficiency not just in the past or in the future, but in the now.

I was teaching once at a church, giving my testimony and saying that I had a forgiven past and a certain future. I was asking the group questions, and they were giving the "right" answers—the typical evangelical answers. Past and future. Past and future. That really is the Christian scene, isn't it? I don't intend any condemnation, but our sense of certainty is in the past and the future, and we have a sense of nothingness in between, in the present. So we fill it up with activity. What else can you do? But Jesus is the present. He gathers all up in the now.

One time Jesus took His inner circle (Peter, James, and John) with

Him to the top of a mountain and He was transfigured (Mark 9). When they came down, they found the other disciples in trouble. They were trying out their healing ministry on a boy, only they weren't getting any results.

The father of the boy just said what was on his heart: "These guys can't do anything."

Jesus immediately moved in and said what could happen to those with faith. And the man, in utter honesty, responded, "I believe; help my unbelief." That is one of the most honest statements in Scripture. "I believe; help my unbelief."

That wavering faith is true of all of us. We have areas in our lives where we haven't yet experienced the saving work, the present tense of Jesus Christ. How precious it is to be brought back to a sense of His presence. And with that sense of His presence comes the knowing of His sufficiency.

It surprises us when we see the answer is a Person. The answer is always a Person. And when we understand that the answer is a Person, it isn't quite as critical for us to have a temporal solution. We are content with His presence. Sometimes God gives us a temporal solution along with a sense of His presence. But often there is no temporal solution. God says to us, "My grace is sufficient for you." There is a sense of companionship, we and God, whereas previously there was only a sense of desperation: "How can I handle this? What will rescue me?"

We move from unbelief to belief, to the sense of the power and the presence of the Almighty One, surrounding us as a fortress, bringing us life within, a peace that passes all understanding.

It's like a woman said to a friend of mine, "I have a real peace about this situation I am in."

"Tell me about your peace," my friend asked her.

"I can't," she said.

He replied, "Then you probably have it."

It passes understanding. In this woman's situation there had been real trauma, but because of her sense of the power and presence of Jesus Christ in the situation, it wasn't quite as critical that the situation be resolved immediately. "I am your total sufficiency."

It's so important to know that we don't have any more spiritual needs (Ephesians 1:3). We don't need any more life. We don't need any more spirituality. We don't hunger and thirst in our spirit. He who said, "I am the life," has come to dwell within us. He has already satisfied our hunger. He is our total sufficiency. We are free to be preoccupied with God's world and His work, because we have been released from a preoccupation with ourselves.

17

The Holy But

People always live after the but. The word, I mean: *but*. Go out and listen to people talk. Everyone lives after the but, whether they're Christians or not. I don't care what they say first, before the but. It's after the but that you hear what they really believe.

"Sam's a nice guy. We're lucky to have him as a pastor. But..." Now we're going to hear what they really think about Sam.

"But he talks too much."

"But his sermons are a bit dry."

"But my momma was sick and he never visited."

We're always living after the but. Unfortunately, Christians typically put the wrong things before and after the but. We put the God stuff before the but and our situation or feelings after the but. We say things like:

"Well, I know God loves me, but it doesn't seem like it. Everything is falling apart."

"I know God is my sufficiency, but I don't really have what I need."

"I know that God promised me wisdom, but all I have is confusion."

You do that, and where are you living? You're living in the junk. You're living in the circumstance. It's got you. The only thing you can hope for is a change in the circumstance. And if that doesn't come, you're up a creek. But even if it does, you still haven't learned to live out of the life of

God within you. Satan doesn't care how much God-talk we use, as long as we put it before the but.

I have a name for putting God after the but, where He belongs. I call it the "Holy But." Jesus used the Holy But in the Garden of Gethsemane. My paraphrase of His famous prayer is: "Father, I don't want to be separated from You. If it's possible, let Me out of it. In fact, this is so heavy on Me right now that my soul feels very depressed…

…yet…

…nevertheless…

…BUT…

…not as I will, but as You will."

That's the Holy But. The Holy But is a bridge. It picks you up from where you're stuck and moves you into faith. If we didn't have the negative in life, we'd never exercise faith. You don't deny the negative, because it's real and it's what prompts your move into faith.

"I feel awfully weak, but God is my strength."

"I'm sorrowful, but God is my peace."

"I'm in pain, but Christ is my sufficiency."

"I want to watch this TV show, but Christ in me wants to take time to listen to this person's hurt."

The Holy But moves you from the level of soul, from thoughts and feelings (which are perfectly normal reactions to life's situations), to the level of spirit, to faith, to allowing Christ to respond to situations through you with His life. The situation is the same, but you have shifted on the inside.

That's what happened with Jesus in the Garden. He didn't deny the situation. He didn't deny His thoughts and feelings, which felt overwhelming. But He chose to live from the Father rather than from His feelings. He turned the situation, which never did change for Him, into our salvation.

To operate the Holy But, we have to put the stuff first and God's truth last. You can't always change the stuff, but you can change whether you're going to receive it or not. What comes after the but is what you have received.

David understood the Holy But. Listen to how he starts Psalm 13:

> How long, O Lord? Will You forget me forever?
> How long will You hide Your face from me?
> How long shall I take counsel in my soul,
> Having sorrow in my heart all the day?
> How long will my enemy be exalted over me?

Mercy me. Quite a circumstance, isn't it? This is dark. This guy is in trouble. Then he starts to beg.

> Consider and answer me, O Lord my God;
> Enlighten my eyes, or I will sleep the sleep of death,
> And my enemy will say, "I have overcome him,"
> And my adversaries will rejoice when I am shaken.

Terrible situation isn't it? What's the next word?

> But I have trusted in Your lovingkindness;
> My heart shall rejoice in Your salvation.
> I will sing to the Lord,
> Because He has dealt bountifully with me.

But. But. But. But. His situation hasn't changed. What's changed? Where he's living from. The but changed him. The but moved him from "How long…" to "I have confidence in the Lord."

What pushed David to make that shift? His circumstance did. That's the importance of the stuff below the line. It's because of the stuff that we exercise the faith that brings Christ's life in us into play.

Paul, too, understood the Holy But. He wrote in his second letter to the Corinthians:

> We have this treasure in earthen vessels, so that the surpassing greatness of the power will be of God and not from ourselves; we are afflicted in every way, but not crushed; perplexed, but not despairing; persecuted, but not forsaken; struck down, but not destroyed; always carrying about in the body the dying of Jesus, so that the life of Jesus also may be manifested in our body (4:7-10).

Paul was living after the but. He put the trouble in front of the but and God, or God's perspective, after the but. Did that change the fact that he was afflicted, perplexed, persecuted, and struck down? Not at all. He continued to experience those things. But where was he now taking his life from? "The life of Jesus…" He moved within himself.

Because we know the truth and live from the truth doesn't mean the external situation is going to change. But *we* are changed. The Holy But moves you from the circumstance to the solution, and that solution is a Person. It moves you from without to within, the outer to the inner, the temporal to the eternal, from looking below the line to looking above the line.

Paul said that he was "always carrying about in the body the dying of Jesus"—that's the seen and temporal perspective—"so that the life of Jesus also may be manifested in our body." That's the unseen and eternal perspective. In the seen and temporal realm, Paul was being persecuted and afflicted. *But* in the unseen and eternal realm, the life of Christ was flowing out through him.

The Holy But always changes your perspective on a situation from external to internal. Regardless who you might want to say is the origin of it—Satan or God—you take that situation back to the Person within you and get God into it.

"What are You about, God? It looks like the devil, but what are You about, God? My child is rebelling, but what are You about, God? I lost my job, but what are You about? My husband left me, but what are You about?" We somehow come back to say, "But God, You're in this." We're not talking about cause; we're talking about God being in it. He is our Source. We go within.

Most of us want to escape our circumstances because we don't know how to operate the but. If we don't know inner life, we want to escape. But if we know the inner life, we understand that the Christian life is us living in the same situations everyone else lives in, but we live differently.

No one can chain your spirit. No one can make a slave of you internally. Satan is off-limits there. Your spirit and the Holy Spirit live in perfect harmony. When something is in perfect harmony, it runs smoothly. It's quiet. It's at rest.

The soul is seldom in harmony. If you get to a point where your soul is in harmony, just enjoy it, because it isn't going to last long. What's going on in the soul, the body, and the world is confrontation and strife. We are pulled and tugged. Our feelings fluctuate. Sometimes we're as high as a kite and sometimes we're dragging the floor.

That's where the difference is seen in our lives. Apart from Christ, we can't respond to life's circumstances differently than anyone else. If we try, we'll only produce something phony. Only Christ can be this life, but He doesn't operate His life in a spiritual vacuum. He operates His life in human beings. He operates it in you and me.

We experience the dying of Jesus when we say no to the stuff. "I realize that the situation is bad. I realize that my thoughts are sour. I realize that my feelings are discomforting. *But* I don't draw my life from my circumstances or my thoughts or my feelings. Christ is my life, and He is my sufficiency this very moment." The life of Jesus is manifested in our body when we say yes to faith.

Sometimes we allow the circumstances of our lives to produce doubt in us concerning our relationship with the Lord.

"Why don't I sense the presence of the Lord like he does?"

"Why doesn't God ever speak to me like He does to her?"

"Why doesn't He ever do with me like He does with him?"

Have you ever said those kinds of things? I used to say them. I couldn't see God's purposes in my life's stuff. I concluded that my brand of stuff meant I wasn't functioning right or else such and such wouldn't have happened to me. I was still focusing on the temporal situation, either blaming God or someone else.

We can sit around and blame if we want to, but we'll never move on to the deep things of God. I can blame my father for not inviting me up on his lap and cuddling me and talking to me, instead of hiding behind the newspaper. I can say that I'm like I am because of my "mean old daddy," but I'll stay stuck right there. How my father treated me may be a below-the-line fact, but that doesn't operate above the line. It doesn't determine who I am in God's eternal realm.

We won't get free of anything in our past or present, nor have peace with anything, no matter how horrible it is, until somehow we take it back to God for His answer. We all need to apply the Holy But to our past. "You meant it for evil, but God meant it for good." In a real way, below the line, our circumstances can be very good or very bad. But there is also a sense in which our circumstances are neutral. *It's how we take them in that counts.* Where we are living always comes after the but.

Our main objective now is not to manipulate the seen and temporal realm, to make it as we want it, but to interpret the seen and temporal by means of the unseen and eternal. The Holy But is what does it.

The temporal stuff truly is happening. Don't try to get anyone to deny what's going on. Why get them to deny a fix that God has engineered in order that God might fix them? Why not instead cause them to see the comfort that comforted you when you were in the fix God engineered to fix you? Everyone else is giving them a technique to try to cope with their fix. But they are still in their fix. You may be the only one who sees what God sees, who knows the comfort that comforts a person when they are afflicted, perplexed, persecuted, and struck down.

There is a battle of faith when we operate the Holy But. However, once that battle is won in an area or circumstance, it is won. After Jesus's Holy But experience in the Garden, the soldiers came to arrest Him.

> Simon Peter then, having a sword, drew it and struck the high priest's slave, and cut off his right ear…So Jesus said to Peter, "Put the sword into the sheath; the cup which the Father has given Me, shall I not drink it?" (John 18:10-11).

Once the battle of faith is settled—once you don't deny the circumstance but come to the place of your permanent victory, to where the life is—you can go through what God gives you to go through. I'm not saying you can go through anything, because my anything may not be your anything. But whatever He gives you to go through, He can go through it as you.

How you go through is a witness to and salvation for others. You don't go through like the world goes through. You go through in the power of the Spirit and in the joy of the Lord. You understand that you're not alone. You understand that your life counts.

The key is agreeing with what God says and putting that after the but.

God says we are holy and blameless in His sight (Ephesians 1:4; Colossians 1:22). God didn't ask you, "Are you irreproachable in your sight?" Seldom do we see ourselves that way. He says, "You are irreproachable, you are holy and blameless, in My sight." And He's the one who counts.

You experience victory when you agree with how God sees you. Stop debating with Him: "But…but…but…I know how You see me, but…I know what the Word says, but…" Just agree with how God sees you. "You see me as holy and blameless and irreproachable. Thank you. I'm holy and blameless and irreproachable." You'll be surprised at what happens within you.

As I've said, the verse the Holy Spirit used to quicken my inner being and give me my first real word on how to live the Christian life was Galatians 2:20. The King James Version reads:

> I am crucified with Christ: nevertheless I live; yet not I, but
> Christ liveth in me: and the life which I now live in the flesh
> I live by the faith of the Son of God, who loved me, and gave
> himself for me.

Have you ever asked anybody to read that verse and put his or her name in there? It's amazing what it will do for you. "Dan has been crucified with Christ. Nevertheless, Dan lives. No, Dan doesn't. Christ lives in Dan." Get the difference? It'll smack you right in the face. Do it for yourself.

Most people want a confirmation of God's truth first, and then they'd be willing to confess it. They want seen and temporal evidence. That's the way the world works. The world says, "You act holy, and we'll call you holy." God says, "Say you're holy, and I will bring that forth in the seen and temporal." The Father is telling us, "Say I'm in you and through you and as you, and I'll show you I am. Just whisper it in your spirit, 'I am.' I'll show you that you *are*. In all My beautifully manifested variety, I'll show you the I AM in you. But you must affirm before I will confirm."

Every time there's a doubt about that affirmation, you just repeat it. Repeat affirming what God has already confirmed to you. "I don't look like it, but I *am*. I don't feel like it, but I *am*. I don't think I am, but I *am*." Then God says, "That's good. That's good."

I find it helps to speak the truth out loud so my ear can hear it. I did that when I first heard who I was in Christ. I used to stand shaving and I'd say out loud who I was in Christ and who Christ was in me. I had so many thoughts that challenged my confession and so many actions that didn't look like what I was saying, so my ear needed to hear the truth, because to simply think it wasn't enough for me. The minute I had one truthful thought, I'd have two or three more following right along behind that said, *That thought's a lie. That thought couldn't be true.* But when I said it out loud, it made a lasting impression on my ear—really, on my spirit. Nobody else heard me say it, but I heard me say it. That's what I needed.

It also helps to say it to someone else. It's a blessing if you have a spouse or a friend who understands you and what God is doing in your life, who won't think you're crazy to say what your inner heart senses and knows is true. If you have a friend like that, you'll get a confirmation back, won't you? You'll get a word back from that friend: "I believe that with you. That's right. I'll take a stand with that. Yes. That's God's truth."

In a sense, the only way we know God's truth about one another is to hear each other say it. "Dan, I have been crucified with Christ. I am dead to sin. It is no longer I who live, but Christ lives in me…" That's true, isn't it? That is the absolute truth. But you don't look dead. You don't look like you're freed from sin. You don't look like Jesus Christ is the one living in you. Nevertheless, that statement is the verbal witness out of our inner being. By faith we believe that about ourselves and about each other.

These are some practical things with me. I don't teach a lot of things that many people would call "practical." To some, it's all a bunch of theory. But when you live it, when you know it, when you experience it, it's practical. In any case, the Holy But is very practical. And I recommend these few steps to solidify God's truth in your heart.

I was talking to a group in a region of the country that was going through an economic downturn. It was the year after I had struggled with cancer, so I could relate to them going through some hardship. I said to them: "Some of you have trouble with permanent employment or the kind of employment you'd like to have. Your finances are precarious. Those are real life experiences that might temporarily pull us down. But the practical thing is that God has shown us another way of looking at life, from His point of view. If we are going to live out of the life of Another, then we have the privilege of looking at life as that One looks at life."

That is our place of permanent victory and rest. We see what God sees. We say what God says. We live as He lives through us.

18

Temptation: A Faith Opportunity

In chapter 7, I introduced "the swing," the ceaseless oscillation of our soul between good and bad thoughts and feelings. We all try to stop the swing but find that we can't because God put it into operation as a prerequisite for faith choices. Until we're reconciled to that fact, we fight the swing. And we fight one particular aspect of the swing the most: temptation. But to be at rest in God, we must also be reconciled to this fact: temptation is an integral part of the swing.

When speaking to groups around the country, I usually close my talk on the swing with an illustration from the life of Jesus. It highlights the most troubling part of the swing: temptation, and how it played out in Jesus's life. I have found that what it teaches usually surprises people. In Matthew we read:

> Then Jesus came with them to a place called Gethsemane, and said to His disciples, "Sit here while I go over there and pray." And He took with Him Peter and the two sons of Zebedee, and began to be grieved and distressed. Then He said to them, "My soul is deeply grieved, to the point of death; remain here and keep watch with Me" (26:36-38).

On what level is this going on? The soul level. That's what Jesus says. He's experiencing something that produces sorrow in Him. Is this feeling contrary to what Jesus knows is God's will for His life? Absolutely. He has known and announced that the cross is God's will for His life. But at this moment His feelings are in a different place.

Jesus's swing is swinging toward what below the line we would call the "evil" direction. His feelings are being pulled away from God's will for His life. But Jesus wasn't like I was for so many years, because He didn't fall on His knees and say, "Oh, God, forgive Me for that feeling." He just accepted it. Why? Because in His humanity, He was meant to be capable of that feeling. And it wasn't a sin to have it.

I used to think, *If I really loved God, how could I have a feeling like that? There must be something wrong with me.* But had Jesus sinned? What if you had done it? Would you have sinned? If not, then why do you ask God to forgive you of those things? Why do Christians ask to be forgiven for temptation? We feel guilty for even feeling a certain way.

That's the devil's trick, isn't it? He says, "Aha! See there! You're having those feelings!" He's the accuser of the brethren. His trick is declaring, "You shouldn't have that feeling." In other words, he is saying that you, the vessel, ought to be God and not human.

At this point the tempter is sending Jesus some major feelings and thoughts, and they're getting a pretty strong hold on Him.

> And He went a little beyond them, and fell on His face and prayed, saying, "My Father, if it is possible, let this cup pass from Me" (26:39a).

Surely now He's stepped over the line. Surely now He's committed sin. It's no longer just a feeling, now He's talking about not wanting to do it!

But has He sinned yet? Would you have sinned yet?

Of course, we always protect Jesus by saying, "He never sinned." And He didn't. But a whole lot of believers think they've sinned when they go this far. When we have a thought that doesn't coincide with the will of God, we say, "I must be out of the will of God. I need to be forgiven." But Jesus didn't ask to be forgiven.

Why might you have thought you had sinned? Because it seems like you're going against the Lord's will. But have you gone against it? No, you haven't. You're just thinking about it. You're questioning it. But you haven't gone against it.

Let's take a brief detour and see how James explained this process in his epistle, starting in verse 1:12:

> Blessed is a man who perseveres under trial [or temptation—it's the same word in the Greek]; for once he has been approved, he will receive the crown of life which the Lord has promised to those who love Him.

The temptation proves us. It is not outside of but rather an integral part of God's plan for us. Verse 13:

> Let no one say when he is tempted, "I am being tempted by God"; for God cannot be tempted by evil, and He Himself does not tempt anyone.

God can't be tempted by evil. So where is our place of security? It's in God, isn't it? It's in the union of our spirit with His Spirit. Verse 14:

> But each one is tempted when he is carried away and enticed by his own lust.

That's just being tempted. It's not sinning. This is when your swing is going way over to the "evil" side. It isn't hanging limp. It's way over on the evil side. You're thinking it and you're feeling it. Your swing is clanging on the evil bell. Clang, clang, clang, clang. But that's just being tempted. Verse 15a:

> Then when lust has conceived, it gives birth to sin...

How does lust conceive? Union. When you join yourself to it. When do male and female produce a child? When they join themselves together. Life doesn't come out of a thought or a feeling. Life comes out of a choice. So until you make that choice, until you join yourself to it, you haven't sinned yet. Neither had Jesus. We see that as He completes verse 39 in Matthew 26:

> "My Father, if it is possible, let this cup pass from Me; yet not
> as I will, but as You will."

What you join yourself to comes after the *yet* or the *but*. That's the Holy But again. Your truth—what you are believing and choosing—always comes after the but. Jesus said His temptation first, then, "but God." "Not as I'm thinking, not as I'm feeling, but as You will." Where you really are in your experience comes after the but.

After Jesus returned to the disciples and found them sleeping,

> He went away a second time and prayed, saying, "My Father,
> if this cannot pass away unless I drink it, Your will be done"
> (26:42).

It's settled now, isn't it? In verse 39, it was, "I'm sorrowful. Is there another way?" But now during the second time with the Father, He just says, "If it can't be any other way, then let it be." Verse 44 says He went away a third time and said the same words.

It doesn't hurt your ears to hear the truth. As long as truth remains on the thought level, you're going to have many kinds of thoughts. But once the Spirit of God in you selects the thought, and it becomes an expression of your mind through the mouth, then it's like Paul said: we believe with our heart but we confess with our mouth. So Jesus spoke that word: "If this is the only way it can be, then let it be that way." At that point He's committed to it.

This is a hypothetical statement, of course, but if Jesus hadn't known who He was in His deepest identity, it appears that He would have taken His validation from His soul and He wouldn't have gone to the cross. If His soul and the temptation had been the deepest reality to Him, He would have had to say, "I've got to do what My feelings and thoughts tell Me to do." He had a deeper reality, though. He didn't have to do what His feelings and thoughts told Him to do. He could do what the inner person in Him knew He had to do.

The only person capable of doing that, though, was not Jesus in separation but Jesus in spirit union with the Father. It was the Father doing it through Him. Jesus was an expression of the Father. Jesus and the Father were one. So Jesus's point of reference was that spirit union. The point of origin of His life was the Father. If His point of reference had been His soul, He'd have probably said, "I've got to find another way."

The deepest, truest aspect about anything is what's going on in the spirit. When God pushes you and me into spirit reality, we're in the realm of knowing. And there's one thing about your knowing: it doesn't make any noise or inner soulish turbulence. Knowing just is. Your soul makes all kinds of noise. It disturbs you. It disturbed Jesus. But when you know who you are, it really doesn't matter what's going on in the external, in the soul and body and outer world.

In the Garden of Gethsemane, Jesus's humanity was being pulled and tugged and drawn by temptation, but He never made any confession of guilt or took any condemnation. He knew this is God's natural process, and that without that process, He wouldn't ever get to the Holy But.

It's as if He testified, "Here's what I'm thinking and feeling...but I'm not that. I'm not what I'm feeling. I'm not what I'm thinking. I'm at a place within Me where I know the Father, and I live out of whom I know." Temptation, then, was a necessary prerequisite for the operation of Jesus's faith.

You are meant to be tempted or there could be no such thing as faith. I'm not saying you are meant to fall to temptation. But you are meant to stand between those two trees, just like Adam and Eve did, and say, "God said don't eat. Satan said eat. And I'm free. What will I do?" You are meant to be there. God created beings that He has determined will operate by freedom, choice, and faith. And we are meant to have the consequences of our free choices.

The spiritual tension in our life didn't start until we were born of the Spirit. Once we were born again, we were catapulted into this tension between flesh and Spirit. Our flesh, humanity operating independently of God, takes its orders from the external. The Holy Spirit, in union with our spirit, gives us a new desire: God's desire.

Once you become a spiritual person, you're in that tension between the two. We always want to get rid of the tension. I'll tell you when there wasn't any tension: when we were dead in trespasses and sins. Thank God for tension. It means you're alive in your spirit. No wonder James said, "Consider it all joy when you have various temptations," because that's where your spiritual growth and stability occurs. We grow by learning to operate out of spirit knowing rather than soul thinking and feeling. As we do, we are for the praise of His glory.

There is a stage in which we pray, as in the Lord's Prayer, "Lead us not into temptation." You don't usually send spiritual babes into harm's way. They aren't ready for it yet. But eventually we come to a place in life where we know that temptation is an intended part of life. When we're tempted, we recognize that we're in an engagement for God—an engagement in which we're not meant to fall but to be victorious. But we can't be victorious unless we know how to be victorious. That's why we have to know that we're dead to sin. And that's why we have to know the difference between soul and spirit.

We need to understand that God gives Satan the privilege of operating in various ways below the line in our lives. Just as we saw in Peter's life (when Satan asked permission to sift him like wheat) and in Paul's life (with his thorn in the flesh, a messenger from Satan), God hasn't declared your soul or your body completely off-limits to Satan. Only one place is off-limits, where we are safe. That's our spirit union. You and I can go around shouting all we want that Satan doesn't have any right in our soul, but it's amazing how he knows what his rights are and how he keeps showing up. He keeps troubling us there. He keeps being God's agitator, because even Satan can't escape being under the sovereignty of God.

Temptation is absolutely necessary in our life. If we see that, we see Satan is no longer our enemy because we're seeing him from God's point of view as a necessary prerequisite in our life for faith activity. When you're no longer doing battle with Satan, you've pulled the stinger out of him. Not that we start calling evil good or we start denying Satan. I'm not saying that at all, because Satan is alive and present. But Jesus disarmed him at the cross (Colossians 2:15). He no longer has any power over you. The minute you see that he no longer has any power over you, isn't it amazing—you stop acting as if he has power over you.

So Satan, our flesh, and the world will continue to tempt us. Satan wants us to take condemnation for just being tempted. All too often we accept it. "I shouldn't have that thought. I shouldn't have that feeling."

Do you know when you won't have any of those feelings or thoughts? It's when they look down in that box and say, "Doesn't he look natural?" But that's not the solution.

The solution is to take this beautiful person of yourself—made in the image of and in union with God to be a "faithing" person—and learn how God designed you to operate in this freedom you have. What we discover, is that our choices can come from our place of security, from our union with Christ.

How do we learn to operate in our freedom? There isn't a quick answer. But there is an answer. It's learning how to hear the Spirit of God in you as He speaks to you. He speaks to each one of us differently, because each one of us is different. And you will follow His voice because that is where your heart is.

In the union of Spirit with spirit there is no noise. Those two spirits are alike, so there's a calmness, a unity. Tension, disturbance, and noise aren't there. External stimuli get our thoughts and feelings stirred up, though, and the tempter or our flesh will use that stirring to pull us out from that safe place of our spirit.

Jesus said, "My sheep hear My voice." Though that voice is quiet, we learn to distinguish it from all the hubbub in our soul. His voice will gently remind us that we are dead to the enticements to our soul. We're dead to that old call. So when temptation calls, we just hang up. "I used to be married to you; now I'm married to Another, and I'm dead to you. Goodbye."

We're dead to sin, but the tempter isn't dead to us. He isn't meant to be dead to us as long as this seen and temporal realm exists. You and I are meant to be set in a tension, the creative tension that temptation produces for faith responses.

We can spend our lives trying to hide and have very few faith experiences, or we can get out in the forefront and recognize that this is the way life works. In response to temptation, we learn to say, "I'm not meant to be controlled by my feelings and my thoughts. I'm married to Jesus, and the only life that I want to have expressed through me is the life of my Husband."

Life is a schoolroom. God wants us to become safe in every circumstance, in every situation. Whether that will all be accomplished isn't the point. Let's not worry about that. We're in the school of Christ. We are simultaneously perfect and complete, and we are in the process of being sanctified. We're being wooed back to Him in the different areas of our life. God wants to teach us His sufficiency in every area of our life so that we rest securely in Him. He is going to run His lessons by us again and again until we get it straight. We have to learn that we are knowers. Each of us must dare to live out of, "I know this to be true. I don't feel it. I don't think it. But I know it to be the truth."

God doesn't have to run His lessons by us endlessly, though. You have to learn the same lesson only once. Once you've learned, you've learned. Then you can count it all joy when He puts those situations into your life that cause you to step back and say, "I'm not what I'm feeling; I'm not what I'm thinking. I'm the precious expression of the living God who wants only what's best in this situation, who wants only what's best for this other person. So I lay down what my outer self wants for what He wants. Because that is the deepest desire of my heart."

19

Hearing God

The story is told of George Rodriguez, a famous Mexican bandit in the early 1900s, who would slip across the Texas border and rob banks. The Texas Rangers could never catch him. One day when George robbed a bank, a ranger spotted him, followed him back to a Mexican village, and saw him enter a small café. The ranger walked in, drew his pistol, and put it right to George Rodriguez's head.

"George, we've been trying to catch you for months," the ranger said. "You've robbed all the banks along the Texas border. If you don't tell me where the loot is, I'm going to blow your head off."

Now, there was a problem: George didn't understand a word of English. But there was a little boy there who spoke both Spanish and English. So he went over and told George what the ranger said.

George replied in Spanish to the boy, "Tell him to go to the center of the city, face north, go to the well, and count down seven stones inside it, where he'll find a loose stone. Behind it is all the loot I took from the Texas banks."

The boy smiled, turned to the ranger, and said, "George Rodriguez said that he has lived a good and happy life and is prepared to meet his Maker."

It's so important what we hear and how we receive what we hear. You have a heart for God. Along with it, you hear His voice. Jesus said, "My sheep hear My voice." It's a dangerous thing to go around saying you don't, because Jesus said, "My sheep do." Because we are His sheep, we hear.

One night while leading a small group, I asked, "We all hear God's voice, don't we?" Everyone in the group answered, "Yes."

Then I added, "But I have no doubt that hearing is different for each of you than for someone else." They all heard from God, but differently, and each one had come to a faith conclusion that when God spoke to them, they heard Him.

Don't just read the Bible. *Listen for God.* The Word of God is of absolute importance. Equally important is the direct word of His Spirit to your spirit. Learn to distinguish His inner voice when He speaks to you. The kingdom of God is within you. It's the Father's good pleasure to give you the kingdom, but for now it is within you. You experience the kingdom as you learn to hear the voice of God as He speaks to you.

He speaks to each one of us differently, because each one of us is different. Sometimes people ask me, "How do you hear God?" I don't tell them. I don't intend that in a mean way. Anytime a speaker talks about God, though, people think he has some kind of special insight on God. I'm no different. I used to run up to discover what somebody's secret was or how they heard God. If they told me, I would say, "I'm going to try that."

But God speaks to us the way we personally understand His voice. So if I tell people how I hear God, and they're not sure how they hear God, what are they going to do? They are going to think that I've got the way to hear God. I've got the way that *I* hear God. I don't have the way *they* will hear God. You can mislead someone if you say, "This is the way God speaks to you." I just encourage them to believe that God speaks to them, because He does speak to them.

I don't try to define how you will know God's voice. It could be 50 different ways. He may speak to you through another person. He may speak to you through the written Word. He may speak to you through a circumstance. Most often it will probably just be His Spirit speaking to your spirit, not just telling you what to do, but saying, "I love you" or "I'm happy to have you as My child" or "I'm already pleased with you."

When He speaks, you'll know it. I want you to become comfortable with how God usually speaks to you. Then go with it. When you hear

His voice or sense His nudge, go with it. That movement will lead to the next movement, which will lead to the following movements that you and He make together.

An acquaintance of mine, a surgeon, gave his medical practice to two young doctors and went to Kenya as a missionary. He said, "I'm going over there to serve the black man the way the black man has served us for 400 years."

At the time I thought, *What is that guy doing? He's crazy.*

Later, I said to my wife, "You know, that's what everybody thought about us when I quit my job to go around teaching about union with Christ."

"What are you going to do?" they asked.

"I'm going to preach and teach because God told us to," I answered.

"How are you going to live?"

"God's going to take care of us."

They were scratching their heads. "Dan and Barbara have lost their minds," they said.

But God speaks, and you know it. *We* knew it.

Someone will object, "It's too dangerous to tell people to learn to identify the inner voice and go with it."

Yes, it is dangerous. That's what I'm telling you, though, because that's the way God has set up His kingdom. It's an inner kingdom. He has joined Himself to our spirit, the deepest part of us. He wants to manifest His life through us. He does that most fully when we learn to hear His voice and obey it. I'm not putting down the written Word. I'm trying to elevate the indwelling Word.

When we think about it, we realize that learning to hear and follow God's voice is, in reality, the least dangerous way to live. How could you possibly be safer—to yourself and to others—than as someone who is truly led by the Spirit? His way is always the way of love. That makes you the safest person you could be.

Of course, Satan wants to say, "You couldn't hear Him if He shouted in your ear." Or when you say you've heard God, Satan will say, "How do you know those weren't your own thoughts?"

I asked that exact question once to a precious sister I often taught with.

She replied, "Because I don't really have a desire to hear another voice." She didn't mean she was incapable of hearing Satan's temptation. She just meant that because she knew her heart was for God, she had settled in her heart that when she had a thought as to a course of action or a prompting, she was going to take that as from God.

It's the same way with all of us. It's a faith thing. We decide we've heard from God. You can't explain that, and if you could, people would question your sanity. But you've decided that, and I say to you, "You've heard from God; operate on that."

Now, you might say to me, "I did, but the results weren't pleasant." And I say, "So what?" For far too long we've decided what the will of God was or whether we heard God's voice on the basis of the result—whether it worked out pleasantly or unpleasantly. The result is God's business. You hear His voice and obey it.

You will likely say, "What if I don't hear correctly?"

I'll admit that's a possibility, but don't be tripped up by it. Otherwise, how are you ever going to learn? When a little tot stands up and is about to take its first steps, Momma and Daddy run get the camera to record the glorious moment. The baby is wobbling, trying to get his equilibrium, and the parents are a few feet away saying, "Come on. Come on. You can do it." Everybody is ready for the baby to take the first step. What usually happens? The kid falls flat. But nobody notices that. They say, "Get up. Come on." He gets up, tries it again, and falls right back down. "Come on. Get up. You can do it!"

I've never heard anybody, after seeing their baby fall down the first time, say, "Uh-oh. I guess you'll never walk. You tried once and fell. You'll have to crawl the rest of your life."

Wouldn't it be something if all of us adults were still moving around the house on our hands and knees because somebody told us we'd never be able to walk? We don't do that. It might take a few days for the child to get his equilibrium, but you know that child was made to walk, and you keep affirming that to the child, and you keep believing that yourself. By not focusing on the falling, but staying with what you know is true, you receive what you have believed. That little baby begins to walk.

It's the same with hearing God. Don't worry if you fall. You've got to learn to listen. Making mistakes at first is part of the learning process.

Just like the parents of the baby, God isn't that concerned about you falling. The parents expected the child to fall. Their camera was there, just in case he didn't. If you really get honest about it, though, you know the kid is going to fall for several days until finally that balance does come and he can take those wobbly little steps, and everybody screams and applauds. If you blow it now and then when you're learning to hear God, fine. That's the way I've learned to cook, by throwing out all the ways I didn't do it right. I say, "Well, that didn't work." Eventually you learn how you do it.

So don't worry about falling. Learn to hear how God speaks to you your way. Then follow Him. You will get better advice from His inner voice than you will from the how-to books. They are written from another person's point of view about how they handle things. But that isn't necessarily God's way of leading you.

Trust the Spirit of God. Listen to the Spirit. He is the Teacher. We can trust Him to teach us to hear Him correctly. The Scripture assigns only one Person the role of Teacher, and that's the Holy Spirit (John 14:26; 1 John 2:27). The rest of us are just informers and reporters and illustrators. If we are going to be spiritual people—and we are—we have one Teacher.

I mentioned previously that I was diagnosed with stage-four cancer and had chemotherapy treatments during 1994. The next spring, as I continued chemotherapy, a word began to form within me. It didn't originate with me. I have spoken presumptuous words of faith before, but down inside me, in the way that I understand God speaks to me, I heard this: "When you have a CAT scan, you're going to be clean."

My CAT scan was scheduled for July 1995. I didn't tell the word to anybody. I thought, *I'm not going to say anything like that.* But it wouldn't go away. "When you have that CAT scan in July, you're going to be clean." The word was a little stronger this time, so then I told somebody. The next thing I knew, I told a small group of people. Then I started telling anybody who might be interested. At conferences I got bolder and said, "Yes, the Lord told me that when I have that CAT scan, I'm going to be clean." I began to believe it.

I went to the hospital in July for my last chemotherapy treatment and my CAT scan. The technician put me on the scanning table and, as she was setting me up, said, "We'll just have to pray that you have a nice report."

"Well, my dear, I must tell you something," I replied. "The Lord has told me I will be clean."

About twenty minutes later, from the adjoining control room, she said, "Well, I'm not your doctor, but it's as clean as anything I've ever seen."

The doctor came in later, and I asked him, "What do you call that, Doc?"

"We call it clinical remission," he said.

"I'm going to call it a healing from God!" I realized afterward God didn't use the word *healing*. He said, "You'll be clean."

In the same still, small voice that Elijah heard, the Spirit of God in me had spoken to my spirit. I knew that word didn't originate with me.

My wife wasn't healed of her cancer. I asked her one day, "Barbara, you've had so many prayers prayed for you. Has God ever told you that you are going to be healed?"

"No," she responded.

I don't know why He told me I'd be clean. If I were God, I would have healed Barbara instead. But I use the story of my cancer and healing to illustrate this: the inner word is what is real. Cultivate your inner life. That's where reality is.

Here are three practical points about hearing God. First, more often than not, you're going to hear His voice in the mess. When external circumstances or soul turmoil are doing a number on you, and you don't have any good feelings to draw upon, you will hear His voice. His Spirit speaks directly to your spirit. When nothing in the external, including your soul, validates that, it makes it all the more clear that He's the one speaking.

Second, we can do things to cultivate our ability to hear Him. One is to spend time with Him alone, just listening. I've observed that it's very hard for most Christians to be all alone. We want someone to talk to because when we're talking, we don't have to face ourselves. And when we're talking, we don't have to face God. Prayer is listening as well as talking. It's difficult to listen, though. It's challenging to believe that you actually hear. Take time in silence to listen.

The last point is this: you will do what God prompts you to do. Often when believers learn to trust Christ to live through them, they begin to doubt their motives. "How do I know that this isn't just my selfish desire?" they ask.

Who is the author of that accusation? At this point we're so close to living a spontaneous, Spirit-directed life that Satan wants to challenge us whether we will do what God prompts us to do.

We will. Past experience alone should tell us that. Back when we were trying to live the Christian life from our own effort, we wanted to do what God wanted. We just couldn't, because we hadn't yet learned to live from the Spirit. But our heart's desire was to do His will.

Now that we have learned to live by His inner voice and we aren't striving anymore, we needn't wonder, "Will I really do what God wants me to?"

Our inner man is always in agreement with God (Romans 7:22). Since He called us into His kingdom, we have always wanted to do what He wants. Previously, we just didn't know Him in such a way as to let Him do it through us. Now we do. The more we come to know Him and hear Him, the more we will manifest Him through our spontaneous living.

Your heart is for God. You do hear His voice. And you will do what His voice tells you to do.

20

Making Decisions

Every person's life has a certain habit to it, an everyday flow. We take no serious thought about it, nor are we overly anxious about it. We just get up and do it. We have a job to do or responsibilities to fulfill and we get up and do them. That's where the large majority of life is lived.

Problems seem to arise in two areas, though. The first is that some of this spontaneous flow of life—including major decisions we make—produces disagreeable results. We take certain actions; in return we get unpleasant reactions. Often, looking back (especially in the short- or intermediate-term), we would call them mistakes. We need to know, however, that just because we get what appear to be unpleasant results that doesn't mean we've sinned or missed the mark. It doesn't even mean that we've made a mistake or that we're outside the will of God.

As I was finishing seminary, I began looking for a church to pastor. A church in rural Kentucky invited me to come preach a trial sermon as part of the interview process. I knew that if they wanted me as pastor, I wanted them. At the time, I knew nothing at all about union. I was living as if in separation—living *for* God. I was living from the belief, "You can know the will of God or you can miss the will of God." Naturally, I wanted to be *in* the will of God.

The church hired me, and my family moved to what I'll call Church Number One. It was truly lovely, with a bunch of young people with young children just like ours. The congregation wanted to be involved and was cooperative. We were very happy and content there, but I said to my wife, "Now, Barbara, we're not going to stay here long. You can't do big things for God in a country church. I want to do big things for God, and if you're going to do big things for God, you have to get to the city, where more people live."

So when the first opportunity came to move to a city church, I wanted it. And because I wanted it and it was bigger and it was fulfilling the dream I had, I concluded, "Well, this is the Lord. This is the will of God. I planned for this to be the next step, and here it is."

So I took it and we moved. Barbara cried all the way. We had been there about two weeks when someone knocked on the front door. I opened it and recognized a deacon from the church. He said, "Brother Stone, I've come to talk to you."

"Well, come in," I replied. "Come in. Sit down."

His message could be summarized in one sentence: "I think we've made a mistake."

That conversation was the high point of my time at Church Number Two. It went downhill from there. On a subsequent night, all the deacons gathered at the church to meet with me. I had to sit and listen as they explained why they thought they had made a mistake. To avoid a big church fight, we agreed that I would tell people that when the opportunity arose, I would be moving.

It took a few months, but a friend called from Florida with an invitation from a small church to give a trial sermon. On the way there, Barbara asked, "Dan, how are you going to know if the Lord is in this move?"

I pondered deeply the things of the Spirit, meditated on the Word, and came forth with this profundity: "If they don't have any deacons."

I walked into the church that Sunday morning prepared to give my trial sermon. The church had an old concrete floor, slanted and covered with moisture. I looked out at the congregation; the pews were three-fourths empty. About 115 people showed, and at least 80 of them had to be over 75. A few little kids ran around without parents. They didn't know one thing about church, and their conduct produced chaos. One old man was sitting on the front row who couldn't have heard thunder right beside him. He was in the midst of all these kids climbing the pews and throwing paper wads and tearing up the bulletins. Everyone else was sitting in the back. I said to God, "Come here?"

After the church service I was told, "After lunch we're going to have a meeting with the leaders of the church to find out if you're interested."

"Who's coming to the meeting?" I asked. "Are the deacons coming?"

"We don't have any deacons."

I said to God, "Uh-oh. You've done it to me again."

We moved to Church Number Three and had four of the greatest years we ever had.

Here's the point. Under my old way of thinking, Church Two was a mistake. I had erred, and I probably figured that somehow I had sinned because I had missed the will of God. But let me tell you the truth. Operating the way I operated in those days, I would never have gone from Church One to Church Three. No way would I have gone from that delightful country church to that mess. Besides, I had more people attending the country church than they had at Church Three. Humanly speaking, I would have never gone from One to Three. But I was glad to go from Two to Three! *Very* glad.

For years, under my old way of thinking about good and evil, I thought I had been outside of God's will by going to Church Two. But then I saw this truth: God is in everything. I saw that when I wanted Church One, God said, "You can have it." And when I wanted Church Two, He said, "You can have it." And when I needed Church Three, He said, "You can have it." I saw that Church Two was the place He had wanted me to be at that point in time. I never was out of God's will. But back then I was living by appearances. If it was good, it was God, and if it wasn't working out, it wasn't God. However, all three church experiences were the positive expression of God in my life.

I want you to see that unless you do something heinously wrong, you aren't out of God's will. He uses everything in your life as part of the potter's work. All the potter does is throw the clay back on the wheel and work it again. In my case, God just took that part out and worked it again. He didn't destroy it and throw it away. It wasn't useless to Him. He just worked it again. That's what He does to you. He massages that place, pulls it out, and works it again.

In God's economy, there aren't really mistakes. There are experiences that have unpleasantness in them, but unless the Holy Spirit says so, you haven't sinned. And you haven't missed God's will. You are one with God. You are God's will. He expresses Himself through you. And He uses all of your decisions, just as the potter continually works the clay.

The second problem that arises concerning decisions is this: What if I have to make a quick decision and don't have much time to pray about it? How can the Spirit give me guidance? We handle that problem by believing this: Even in our haste, He is present. Even in the quick decision, He makes it. Even when we are rushed, He is the guidance.

Such circumstances push us farther out on the diving board of faith. To retreat on that diving board is to question whether God in you is able. Instead, we can go out on that springboard, on that faith board, and trust Him. Even if we have to make a decision instantaneously.

After I had been on the road for 15 years teaching union with Christ, a man I had worked with at Georgetown College in Kentucky accepted the presidency of a Baptist college in Virginia. Barbara and I went to his inauguration. On the way there, I said to her, "You know, I'm going to ask some of my old friends if any of them might have a position for me."

Just off the wall like that. I didn't pray, "Lord, do you have anything…" I just said to my friends, "Do any of you guys have anything I can do for a couple of years?" I wasn't even taking it seriously, but I got two job offers, and I accepted one at Samford University in Birmingham, Alabama.

That was in November. As we prepared to move, in the middle of December we found out my wife had ovarian cancer. She had surgery two days after Christmas. Two months before, we didn't have a good health insurance plan. But at Samford I could select an HMO plan that covered preexisting health problems. They provided Barbara with excellent health care for the rest of her life.

I just stood back in amazement, because God threw open that door on what I would call my flippancy. It wasn't serious. It wasn't something I prayed about extensively. But God didn't jump ship just because I was appearing to be flippant. That's not the only time God has acted through such spontaneity.

Take the faith plunge. If you have to make a decision quickly, trust that God is going to make it through you. And once you take that plunge, don't worry about the consequences. Just watch for Him. The consequences can be up and down. If you focus on them, you're drawing your life from the consequences. Draw your life from God instead.

Why is this important? Because so many Christians are hopelessly bogged down, trying to figure out the "perfect will of God" for every decision. Should I go to this college or that college? Accept this job or that job? Buy this house or that house? Go to this church or that church? Order pepperoni pizza or sausage pizza? That sounds ridiculous, but some believers are almost that immobilized trying to discern the will of God. Most believers are at least partially immobilized.

God doesn't want us to live that way. Such thinking arises from a sense of separation: "God is way up there. I'm way down here. Somehow I have to figure out His perfect will." But there is no separation. You and God are one. He lives in you. He lives through you. He guides you.

I'm not discounting here the importance of what I said in chapter 19 about spending time with God and cultivating our ability to hear Him. But Christians become paralyzed because we think it's all about us and our ability to hear. It's not. It's all about Christ. He is the One living through us. If we're available to Him, it's His job to make sure we hear.

We often hear a verse from Isaiah quoted: "'For My thoughts are not your thoughts, nor are your ways My ways,' declares the Lord" (55:8). That was true in its context, in the Old Testament, before the New Covenant and the new birth. Because He has birthed us by His Spirit and has placed His Spirit within us, in union with our spirit, we can say, "My will is His will. My thoughts are His thoughts. My desires are His desires." We can live our lives in spontaneous flow and not be anxious that we have taken a wrong turn.

Someone may say, "But it's hard to get self out of the way."

That's one of those ruts we fall into. We have this rut of self-doubt: "Don't trust yourself!" It's understandable. After all, we've had a long history in which we should distrust ourselves. Our false self, operating independently of God, couldn't be trusted. But we *can* trust the self in which He lives, in union with you. Because that's the way He operates, through you. Just say, "I'm going to say by faith that my self is out of the way." Unless we really decide to act evil, we don't want to make an evil decision. Unless we choose to be disobedient, we don't want to make a selfish decision. So let's believe we don't! Let's trust Him to live His life spontaneously through us, as us.

Because of our union with Christ, we can say, "I'm going to look at myself differently. I'm an antenna. I'm a point of contact. I want only what God wants. I'm His vessel here. I'm His human contact with other humans. So I'm going to believe that He is living through me."

He isn't going to reward our unbelief. He's going to reward our belief. So let's believe that He's operating in our decisions. Because He is.

21

Detached Living

Those of us who write or teach extensively about our union with Christ emphasize *being* over *doing*. And we should. In the context of our spirit union, doing flows from being. But if we're to give Jesus free reign to live His life through us—if we are to truly experience His abundant life—we're going to have to make some choices. One of those choices involves detaching ourselves from a preoccupation with the values of this world.

Most people already have a full pie. Their lives are full. If it's religion we're giving them, if they're halfway interested at all, they'll try to wedge this little piece of religious pie into their already-full life pie, as if it's just part of a whole. Religion is always just part of a whole. Anything beyond a little religious activity has a hard time crowding into our busy lives.

We who know Jesus as our Savior are so busy. In Jesus's parable, we are often "the ones on whom seed was sown among the thorns; these are the ones who have heard the word, but the worries of the world, and the deceitfulness of riches, and the desires for other things enter in and choke the word, and it becomes unfruitful" (Mark 4:18-19).

The people in Jesus's parable were just too busy. That's the world today, isn't it? Good people—believers—are just too busy. "Yes, I love the Lord, but I'm just so busy." So we teachers come along with a slice of religious pie, and people are looking for a slice they can handle, to wedge it in to an already busy life.

I was always glad to have people come to conferences where I spoke. However, I knew that if they were just looking for another wedge of pie that might make life a little happier, a little easier, a little less stressful, then they were missing the point. Jesus isn't offering you another slice of pie. Jesus doesn't have another Band-Aid to patch you up with. He really doesn't.

I'm not talking to people about religion. I'm talking about *life*. And I'm not talking about adding a new piece of pie called "Christ in you, the hope of glory" into your already busy lifestyle. I'm talking about a new lifestyle—not another piece of an already busy life, but something so dramatic that it might call for some of us to completely reorient our lives.

Let's be honest. A lot of what we do isn't necessary. I like what my mother used to say: "I don't try to keep up with the Joneses; I am the Joneses." Well, she really wasn't, but so much of what we race around doing is just us trying to keep up with everybody else.

Being a senior citizen, I realize that it doesn't take as much for me to live on now. But I have the opportunity to watch the upcoming generations, and the truth is I've never seen so much stuff. I go to people's houses where I have to step over all their stuff. They don't have any more closet space. I went to visit some dear friends of mine, and I couldn't hang three shirts in the guestroom closet; it was bumper-to-bumper with dresses. It seems everyone has to have more and more.

There's so much activity for things we don't need in our lives. If we're talking about a lifestyle of living from the unseen and eternal realm, some of us are going to have to make some changes. Otherwise, we're constantly going to be too distracted to ever be in touch with anything but the seen and temporal.

The more we let the world beset us by dictating priorities, the more traps we're going to get into. That's a fact. I simply want you to mull this one over with the Holy Spirit. Do you really need everything you're working for?

I decided a while back that I wasn't going to join the computer age. I was over 70 anyway; what did I need it for? I only needed arithmetic to keep my checkbook balanced. And who needs all these words or the Internet? We have all this information coming, and we haven't yet mastered "You shall love your neighbor as yourself." I'm still working on that one, aren't you? Why do we need all this information? It just bogs us down. Of course, I'm passing on and I recognize that people need to utilize a new technology. But how much does all of this add to our lives—or does it perhaps subtract from our lives?

I find that I give my time to whatever my passion is. It's something I don't have to try to wedge in. I'm willing to give my heart, my life, and my time to my passion. Jesus said, "Where your treasure is, there your heart will be also" (Matthew 6:21). I want my passion to be God.

Repeatedly my attention is drawn in the New Testament to those interesting people who heard Jesus gladly. I know one reason they did: they didn't have any appearances to live on. People who don't hear Him gladly are usually living on appearances and comparisons. "I look better than you look. I live on a different side of town than you do. I've got a different kind of education than you've got. My bank account is bigger than yours. My church is bigger than yours."

But the harlots, tax collectors, lepers, blind, and lame had no appearances. And it didn't bother them that Jesus didn't have any. They were dead and they saw life in Jesus. When you're deceived and distracted, you don't see life. But when you're hungry, you hear gladly.

I want my understanding of Christ being my life to be a lifestyle, not an adjunct. It's not a piece of the pie; it is the pie. And I think that's your heart too. Christ is all in all. We want the all. And we, who are the lame, want to yield the all of us to Him. But we can't do that if we're attached to the world.

Jesus lived His earthly life as a detached person. Not detached from loving people, but detached from the world. He wanted only to do the will of the Father. There wasn't anything in the external realm that could enhance His identity. That's what I mean by detached. Jesus could operate in this world with complete freedom because there wasn't anything in this world that He wanted to possess more than He wanted to be possessed by His Father.

That may be happening in you. Where it isn't, you're in turmoil, because God is going to pry your fingers loose. Whatever thing or person or ambition you're still holding on to, you're in turmoil over, or you will be. You don't have peace in that area yet because there's still something outside of you giving you validity.

In some of my reading I came across a phrase used by the desert fathers, early Christian monks in the first few centuries after Christ. The word in the Greek is *hēsychios,* which is found only a few times in Scripture. It is often translated "to lead a quiet life." Paul told the Thessalonians to "make it your ambition to lead a quiet life and attend to your own business and work with your hands" (1 Thessalonians 4:11). He urged that prayer be made for all men and those in authority, "so that we may lead a tranquil and quiet life in all godliness and dignity" (1 Timothy 2:1-2). In these verses Paul used the word with both an external connotation and an internal connotation.

We may have periods—or at least moments—when we experience a quiet, peaceable life externally. When my wife and I were external persons, we liked to go on retreats because they allowed us to get away for a weekend. We left the kids at home and somebody else cooked for us, so it was different from our ordinary routine. It was quiet. I don't mean the absence of any noise, but the absence of a routine. The retreats were tranquil places.

As we would leave those retreats to head back home, though, the quietness would slowly ebb away. By the time I drove up to the house, I was already reverting to my pre-retreat self. I was going to walk in there and straighten out the kids and reestablish my authority and get my space. I was right back where I was before, because quietness to me was a completely external thing.

We can manufacture quiet for a little while. We may be able to create an external setting where we can occasionally have quiet. But I'm talking about an internal quiet that filters throughout our lives.

The desert fathers sought a quiet inner life. They were men and women who were seeking God. One of the pivotal events that drove them to be desert monks was the Roman recognition of Christianity by Emperor Constantine in AD 313. He made it an officially accepted religion. These men and women knew that was the death knell of New Testament Christianity. Until that time it hadn't been an official religion; it had lived on the perimeter and was always a threat to those in power. Being a Christian involved sacrifice. Christians were persecuted.

But after Christianity became an official religion, there wouldn't be any more sacrifice. It would be the in thing to do. In many places it's still the thing to do today, isn't it? And the more it's the thing to do, the more it becomes an external thing, and the more quickly it dies. As reality moves from internal to external, it moves from life to death.

So these men and women fled. They went to the deserts of Sinai, Palestine, Arabia, and Egypt, just to be with God. They went to make a vocation of what most of us have as an avocation: loving God. They made full-time work of what we treat as a slice of pie in our lives.

Whether they were right or wrong to go off into the desert is irrelevant to the point I'm making. The point is that they went there to develop their spirit oneness with God. They sought God as a full-time vocation.

Instead of pursuing God externally, they pursued Him internally and permitted Him to work His way out through their lives externally. Instead of trying to change their lives from the outside in, they allowed God to change them from the inside out. Like Paul's admonition to the Thessalonians, they sought to lead a quiet life, to mind their own business, and to work with their hands.

Lose your preoccupation with below-the-line things. Focus on what's above the line, the eternal. Jesus said, "Whoever seeks to keep his life [soul-life: *psychē*] will lose it, and whoever loses his life [soul-life: *psychē*] will preserve it" (Luke 17:33). To the person whose eyes are on the temporal, it makes no sense to talk about losing to gain. The only thing that makes sense is gaining more and more of what this world offers.

God's kingdom is not of this world. How do we gain the kingdom? "It is your Father's good pleasure to give you the kingdom" (Luke 12:32 NKJV). "We have received...the Spirit who is from God, so that we may know the things freely given to us by God" (1 Corinthians 2:12).

Freely given. The human, the temporal, wants to take the kingdom violently (Luke 16:16). There must be some way to gain control. The eternal, spiritual side replies, "It's My good pleasure to give it to you."

What are the conditions? To one man Jesus said, "Sell everything and come follow Me." What does that mean to us? Detach. Detach yourself from everything and anything that could give you a false identity. It doesn't mean just to become poor, because there are lots of poor folks who are more preoccupied with money and things than are the rich who already have them. It's God's good pleasure to give us the kingdom. The condition is easy. "Blessed are the poor in spirit"—those who recognize their need—"for theirs is the kingdom of heaven."

He says of this inner pasture that we have, "Come in and dine with Me."

Jesus was in a house in Tyre, and a Syrophoenician woman somehow nudged her way in, uninvited. I doubt if she looked like the religious type. But she was one of those people who knew life when she saw it and pressed right in. She perceived that Jesus was there to meet her at her level. And He did.

As Jesus walked by one day, blind Bartimaeus asked, "What's all that noise?"

"Jesus of Nazareth is passing by," they told him.

"You mean, that guy who heals? Jesus! Hey Jesus, over here!"

"Be quiet!"

"I won't be quiet! Jesus! Jesus!"

He pressed right in. And he went away seeing.

You push right in on Jesus Christ in faith and His heart melts. It's amazing, isn't it? "Sell all that you have and come follow Me." If we want to hang on to this world's stuff, we can have it. But we'll miss God's best if we just go for God's good. And we want God's best.

22

The Gift of Misery

I used to buy my wife clothes as a gift. I wasn't very good at it, and she would soon return them for something she had already spotted that she liked. But the intent of my heart was right. I wanted to give her a gift.

It's lovely to give someone a gift. It's fun. It's exciting to receive a gift, too, particularly if it's something you really wanted and you get it by surprise. It thrills you to get a gift like that. It's wonderful to get a gift from God as well. How many of us have had a gift from Him? All of us. Our salvation, God's Son, His Spirit, our family, our mate and children, if we have them—all are gifts from Him.

There is a gift from God, though, that we often don't recognize as a gift. I call it the gift of misery. I don't know if you see misery as a gift, but it is. Most of us who have been drawn to God, either initially or in a deeper way later on, have been drawn through misery. It was pain, heartache, disappointment, or discouragement that did it.

The truth is that as long as we can handle life, we don't think we need God. We'll tip our hat to Him, but we're doing just fine. Then when we can't handle life, we want Him to get us out of the jam. And He tells us, "I made the jam. Why would I want to get you out of it?"

It's the gift of misery.

I've been through misery. When I lost my wife a few years ago, I went through misery. I went through misery twenty years before in my marriage. I knew that I loved my wife, but I wasn't feeling it. My feelings turned aside temporarily. I was ashamed of that. I hated that. I hated me.

But God was right in the middle of that. He used it in Barbara's life. She stopped having me as her idol. Barbara and I lived together for forty-plus years. The first twenty were fine; the second twenty were precious.

God used misery in my life to cause me to give up on my ability to make my Christian life work. My flesh was legalistic, moral, and proud. I had to learn that, given the right set of circumstances, I was capable of the most heinous act I could think of. I thought I was above that. The gift of misery prepared me for the message of union with Him.

Often in the Scriptures God's primary way of preparing people for Him was the gift of misery. In the Old Testament, Joseph was tossed into a pit by his brothers, sold into slavery, falsely accused, put into prison, unjustly forgotten and left to languish. Eventually he became prime minister of Egypt, but that was a hard route. Humanly speaking, he had a right to be bitter.

When his brothers were at his mercy, however, what was his response? "You meant evil against me, but God meant it for good in order to bring about this present result" (Genesis 50:20). God meant it for good. He used misery in Joseph's life not only to mature him in his faith, but also to bring temporal salvation to his father's household—the entire Jewish nation at that time. Joseph had the same privilege that I had with cancer. He could see the evil of his brothers or he could see the purpose of God. He chose to see the purpose of God.

Many other lives in the Bible illustrate the gift of misery, but I want to focus on three: Moses, David, and Peter. Moses was raised as an Egyptian by Pharaoh's daughter. He grew up in Pharaoh's household. He had the finest Egypt had to offer. Some have speculated that, like Joseph, Moses may have been in line to rule the nation.

Moses became aware that his true heritage was Hebrew, however, and that his people were slaves to the Egyptians. He wanted to be their deliverer. So he went out and killed an Egyptian who was mistreating a Hebrew. He reasoned, "These people are going to see that I'm really with them, that I'm willing to kill for them, that I'm their real leader. They're going to respond to me."

Things didn't quite work out that way. News gets around, doesn't it?

This news got around not only to the Hebrews but also to Pharaoh, who placed Moses on the Egyptian Ten Most Wanted list. Moses was afraid and ran to the wilderness in Midian, the middle of nowhere. The next time we see him, he is sitting by himself at a well.

Moses was miserable. He had been raised in Pharaoh's own household. The whole world was at his fingertips. He had dreamed of liberating his true people, though. Now he had messed that up, as well as forfeiting all the privileges he had grown up with and his future as an Egyptian leader. Talk about regrets. But God was in Moses's messes.

Moses settled down in Midian, got married, had children, and went to work tending sheep. Then one day he saw a bush on fire that wasn't consumed. He went over and heard a voice saying, "Take off your shoes; you're on holy ground."

At this point, forty years had gone by since Moses fled Egypt. And which forty years was it? The middle forty, a man's most productive years. When Moses, in his first forty years, wanted to do a great thing for God, he could have said, "Look at all the clout I have. I'm raised in Pharaoh's house. I can do something for these people. I can get them out from under this burden, maybe out of the land." He saw himself in a place of human power. He didn't need God. He could do it.

Moses was entering the middle third of his life, his most productive time, and God rejected his efforts. He was in misery and he ran. He hid. He made a new life for himself in a strange land. It took him forty years to become content.

Now, he's 80 years old and here comes God's call. God said, "Moses, I've heard My people…I have come down to deliver them out of the land of the Egyptians." Wouldn't you think Moses would be happy? This is what he had waited for. But no, he wasn't too thrilled. He probably thought, *What took You so long? I was ready forty years ago. Where were You then?* But that was his problem. He was ready. He had power. He had influence. That's when God can't use us. When we have all the resources, when we have the power package, when we can do it, then He can't use us. That's a hard lesson to learn, because the world teaches us the opposite.

What did God say to Paul? "When you are at your weakest, I can be My strength in you" (see 2 Corinthians 12:9-10). You can't entirely process this through your brain. It's incredible. It's unbelievable. But the Spirit of God in you resonates, "That's the truth. That's when I can use you, when you don't have anything to bring to Me. That's when I can use you. But as long as you think you are capable and able, you want Me to share My glory with you. And I don't share My glory with any human being in that way." Moses was finally convinced, and God worked through him for His people's deliverance.

Thank God for your misery. It prepares you to be a vessel for His use, for His strength—not yours—to flow through. It doesn't seem to make sense, but in your weakness is your strength. In your misery is your hope. In your death is your life. In your nothing is His everything.

It's amazing how God works. Out of the dung heap grows a rose. Out of misery grows a mighty man of God. Thank God for your misery. Thank God for your pain. Don't attribute it to the devil. If you do, paraphrase Joseph: "The devil meant it for evil, but God turns his tricks on him and works it for good."

Like Moses, David was a man on top of the world. He was the most powerful man in all of Israel. He could do anything he wanted. He loved God and was a man of faith that God had used mightily. But he saw another man's wife and sent to inquire about her. He had more on his mind than inquiring about her.

We all know the story about David and Bathsheba's adulterous affair. After Bathsheba conceived, David plotted to deceive her husband, Uriah, into thinking the child was his. When that didn't work, he had him sent to the front line in battle to be killed.

Now David was guilty of both adultery and murder. Just when he thought he'd gotten away with it, the prophet Nathan came in and told him a story. David was a man after God's own heart, however, and he was aroused to anger by the story—until Nathan revealed that David was the story's villain.

Do you think things could have gotten worse for David? At that point he was about as miserable as it gets. He could have looked around to see if anybody had heard Nathan. "Did anybody hear that? Maybe I can cover this up again." But no. We have the record of David's response in Psalm 51. It is a beautiful psalm of misery:

Be gracious to me, O God, according to Your lovingkindness;
According to the greatness of Your compassion blot out my
transgressions.
Wash me thoroughly from my iniquity
And cleanse me from my sin.
For I know my transgressions,
And my sin is ever before me.
Against You, You only, I have sinned
And done what is evil in Your sight,
So that You are justified when You speak
And blameless when You judge.
(Psalm 51:1-4)

No excuses. Just honesty. Isn't that necessary? What you hide you must acknowledge. What you cover up you must uncover. When did David do business with God? When he was at his lowest point. When do you do business with God? When your life falls apart. Until that happens, we play games with God.

One time I was doing a retreat with a good friend, Bill Hodge. I commented on how many attendees we had had over the years in a certain city and how relatively few actual hearers we seem to have had. Bill said, "People come to hear us because they hope that God will get them out of a fix. We tell them that God made the fix. We ask them, 'Do you want God, or do you want a fix for your fix?'"

We say we want God, but what we really want is a fix. We want an escape. We want the pressure removed. When we don't have anything else to bargain with, though—when we don't have anything to lay before Him but filthy rags, when we're miserable enough—then He's ready to deal with us.

I have a little prayer that I began saying after I read a book by William Barclay, who said that what Jesus said on the cross, "Into Your hands I commit My spirit," was a child's prayer. It was the Jewish version of "Now I lay me down to sleep." That touched my heart—Jesus on the cross, praying his childhood prayer. So I go to bed at night and say, "Lord, into Your hands I commit my spirit." And my life. And my will.

I learned that prayer in misery, after my wife died. I learned that prayer when I would roll over in bed and I was alone. I learned that prayer when a precious memory would come across my mind and there wasn't anyone there to share it with. What was happening? God was drawing me closer in my experience to my true life. *He* is my true life. Thank God for misery.

Unlike Moses and David, Simon Peter wasn't a man of power and prestige. He was a fisherman with a heart for God. He hadn't yet learned what the Lord needed to teach him, though. When Jesus asked the disciples who He was, Peter had been the one to boldly declare, "You are the Christ, the Son of the living God." Jesus said to Peter, "Blessed are you, Simon Barjona, because flesh and blood"—including your human brain—"did not reveal this to you, but My Father who is in heaven" (Matthew 16:15-17). Peter had an "Oh, I see!" moment. He had a revelation. And he couldn't keep quiet about what he had seen.

The next day, though, when Jesus began to talk about dying on the cross, Peter rebuked Jesus: "This can't happen to you. This cannot happen to you." How self-confident! How assured!

Jesus replied: "Get behind me, Satan! You are a stumbling block to Me; for you are not setting your mind on God's interests, but man's" (Matthew 16:23).

Goodness, what a change. Jesus didn't mean Peter was a real devil, but He meant this: "Peter, you savor the things of the flesh, just like Satan does. As you become a true disciple, you're going to see it differently."

The night before Jesus's crucifixion, Peter insisted: "I don't care if everybody leaves you. I'll never leave you." Bless Peter's heart, Jesus knew he meant that. It's just like some of my past boasting, and possibly yours. Jesus knows we mean those words gushing out of us in love and adoration, but He knows we don't have the wherewithal to do it. He understands when we can't back up our boasting or dedication with anything but flesh effort. And He knows that when the going gets rough, we're going to run.

Jesus replied to Peter, "Simon, Simon, Satan has demanded permission to sift you like wheat" (Luke 22:31). Whom do you think Satan asked? He must have asked the Lord. Satan may have asked for you. I want you to see what kind of God you have. In essence, Jesus said to Peter, "I'm not going to jerk you out of the fire. I'm going to let you go through this. But I'm going to pray for you, that your faith won't fail."

I would have said, "Lord, if you don't mind, I'd like a little more help than a prayer." Wouldn't you? "Give me a little more help here."

"No, I'm just going to pray that your faith doesn't fail." That is what God is about, teaching us to live a life of faith.

Peter denied his Lord. When they led Jesus away from one of his trials, Jesus saw him, and Peter wept. Peter was miserable. And the tears of repentance he cried were beautiful tears. Jesus had said, "I pray that your faith won't fail; and you, when once you have turned again, strengthen your brothers." Peter did that. He came back from discouragement, from defeat, from denial of his Lord and Savior. After His resurrection, Jesus appeared to Peter at the Sea of Galilee and three times asked him, "Do you love me?" It was the same number of times that Peter had denied Him. And three times Peter could reply, "Yes, Lord, you know that I love you."

Peter was restored. His confidence was no longer in himself but in His Savior. A few days later the Holy Spirit descended, and the same man who had run away was now full of faith, full of fire, preaching truth to the crowd: "Let all the house of Israel know for certain that God has made Him both Lord and Christ—this Jesus whom you crucified."

"Simon, when you return, strengthen your brothers." God made that possible through the gift of misery.

We've all had experiences in life that we wanted to shove aside, excuse, and deny, instead of using them profitably. But God keeps sending them until we learn our lesson. When we signed on with Him, we gave Him rights and privileges over our lives, to do with as He pleases. Of course, we thought life with God would always be pleasant. That's how we think when we're still babes. But now as we look back we can say, "Lord, that time I was miserable, that's when You became real in my life. That's when in my prayers I was really honest with You. That's when I had to tell You I was really hurting. I had to lay it at Your feet. Out of that old tree stump you caused a new shoot—a new life—to come up. And through that experience You strengthened me. You taught me. You remade my life into that of a disciple who is not above his master."

May God teach us to look at the misery in our lives, the tough times, the hard times, and say, "Yes, but." The Holy But.

Nothing happens to us outside of God's providence and sovereignty. Nothing happens in our lives about which we cannot say, "He meant it for good."

And He works it for good.

23

Poured Out

I'll never forget the time at a conference in Louisville when a friend walked down to the front and testified: "As long as my wife went through my pockets and browbeat me and told me how awful I was, I could resist her. But when she just loved me like I was and made no demands for a change in my performance, I could not resist that love."

Until we became believers, you and I knew nothing at all about God's kind of love. We talked about love. But we didn't know it. Even after we get saved we don't really know it, because we're still living as if in separation, not union. We are still relating to God and others based mostly on feelings. God's love is only as real to us as we feel it. So we are constantly on a roller coaster. We think God loves the same way people love.

But God doesn't love as people do. The New Testament word for God's kind of love is *agapē*. *Agapē* isn't natural to fallen humanity. Friendship love and romantic love are native to humanity. But not *agapē*. God gives *agapē* to us. "The love of God has been poured out within our hearts through the Holy Spirit who was given to us" (Romans 5:5). God gives His love to us in a Person of love, Jesus Christ. Only Jesus can live His love out through us. And love is the only thing He is going to do through us.

Agapē is what is best for the other person's welfare. *Agapē* isn't just sentimental sympathy. It can be the tough word of love as well as the sympathetic. We give what's best for the other. There is no more preoccupation with self. We are lost in what God is doing for the other person.

Of course, we can temporarily allow ourselves to be expressions of the flesh and be takers and takers and takers. But we've walked that path, haven't we? And what did we learn? It was like drinking salt water. We're never satisfied. It never brings us to completion. But when our flesh life is replaced in experience by Christ's life, we begin to be a part of Him living His life through our humanity for His love purposes. Then we can truly say, "I am fulfilling my desires. I'm realizing what life is all about." We experience living waters poured out on a thirsty world.

That's the Christian life.

As Oswald Chambers said, we are poured out wine and broken bread for the spiritually hungry world to eat and drink. And we can't choose to whom we're going to give our life. God does the choosing. He will send some funny people. You wouldn't pick them out. They're not your kind. You're not content with them. You're not compatible with them, but He puts them in your life. They may suck the life out of you, because they're so dry. You're going to think, "If that person calls me again…"

A woman called me one afternoon as Kentucky basketball coach Rick Pitino was about to be interviewed on TV. I thought, *Is she going to get off the phone before he gets on, or am I going to have to turn the volume up?* I began to move her toward ending the conversation.

But that was God's moment. That's what life is about. And I said to myself, *Now, wait a minute. Here's a woman who called to talk to me about how she was driving her car when another car struck hers and her husband was killed. She wants to talk about that. And that's what I'm about, being here for her. What difference does this TV interview make, anyway?*

You have to switch from self to others. That's *agapē*. That's where you participate in God's operation. "Wait a minute," you ask yourself. "What am I here for? Who am I here for?"

Jesus said, "He who believes in Me, as the Scripture said, 'From his innermost being will flow rivers of living water'" (John 7:38). That's why I say, you'd better know that you are already filled. Because those rivers are flowing out of you, and you're going to have a hard time getting a drink for yourself. Your tongue isn't quite long enough to reach those rivers of living water flowing out of you. They are for somebody else. You don't need to drink. You are permanently drunk. You don't need to eat. You're already fat on the Spirit. You're filled.

If we see ourselves as a liability or as hungry and thirsty, we'll say, "I've got to have some of that for me, *then* I'll give some away." But we're getting free of that mindset, aren't we? Above the line, in the spirit realm, we have no need because Jesus has already promised us, "I am your sufficiency. I am your filling."

The fruit we bear is for others. As believers, we bear all kinds of fruit: lemons, limes, and grapefruit, as well as apples, oranges, and tangerines. Some of us are sweet apples and oranges and people come and pick us. Some of us are lemons and limes, and every now and then somebody will say, "I'll pick that one." What kind of fruit we are isn't the point. We're just producing. People do the picking. Don't worry about what your gift is or what your fruit is. It isn't for you. It's for somebody else. They will see in you a particular expression of the life of God, and they will come and take it.

An important part of the life is not worrying anymore about, "What's my fruit? What's my gift? What's my talent?" You just say, "God, I'm Your person." Once you understand that you're His vehicle, you can rest. "God, I'm the perfect expression of You. I may look like a lemon, but there are folks who like lemons." They will see your life and they'll come to you and pick you. "Give me your lemons. Give me your oranges. Give me your apples. Give me your fruit."

You will attract people to the life within you. When I knew only that Jesus died for me, I had to go knocking on doors to tell people about it. When I knew that Christ lived in me and that I was the light of the world, the salt of the earth, His love expression to the world, I could trust that those who see that in me will come to me. They will come to you too. We will give them light.

God breaks through your intellectual barriers and speaks His confirming word to your spirit: "That's who you really are. You're not a liability to Me. You're an asset to Me. But it's not you, it's Me. I have chosen to touch your world by living through you."

There isn't any reason to mistrust or fear your humanity anymore.

You can accept it because you know who is alive in you. He has revealed to you what life is all about. He has counted you faithful to be His inheritance.

God is pleased to love through us just as we are. Paul wrote to the Ephesians: "For we are His workmanship, created in Christ Jesus for good works, which God prepared beforehand so that we would walk in them" (2:10). Are you His workmanship right now? Yes, you are. God in you, where you are right now in your spiritual development, can reach someone else.

Next year you'll be someplace else spiritually, and He will use you then. But He can use you right now. Every day, wherever we are in our walk with Him, He can use us. Because there's someone out there who couldn't take us if we were any deeper. They can take us right where we are. He'll send that kind of person to you.

It's amazing when He sends someone to you. You might think that you don't have an answer for people, but they will pull God's Spirit out of you. They will pull God's answer out of you. I used to hear my wife counsel people. She would give them a lot of my teaching, but not in the right order. It distressed me. I'd say to her, "That part doesn't belong there." But the Spirit of God would use it. Humanly, it was completely disjointed, but it would minister to people. They would hear what God wanted them to hear. She was God's perfect vessel.

No matter how we look externally, we are His workmanship right now. Everything we do, whether work or play, is His opportunity to speak through us. As Paul said, we're ambassadors for Christ. God is making His appeal through us. He's just using our mouth. The burden is off of us. He's talking through us. It sounds like us, but it's Him.

Some are ambassadors to those outside the kingdom. They're going to tell people about the kingdom. Some are ambassadors to those inside the kingdom. Their work is to be an encourager, to speak the truth of the unseen and eternal realm to a brother or sister whose vision is temporarily blocked or blurred. My wife was so good at speaking a word of encouragement.

The world God has sent you to be an ambassador to is your individual world. Don't worry about someplace you can't get to. He has you in your place. That's your world. Even within your town, your world is the people and the situations you come in contact with. If God wants you somewhere else, He'll get you there. If He wants you to be interested in something else, He'll find a way to get you interested in something else. Right now you could ask yourself, "What does God have me interested in?" Those will probably be the very things you're currently doing. "Who does God want me to know?" The very people you know. That's your world. Operate in it. It isn't you, it's God.

That's the Holy Wink. It looks like you, but it's God operating as you.

Let me tell you more about the lady who called before the Rick Pitino interview. She told me, "When the accident took place, I saw two ladies who had pulled off the road, and they were standing together, huddled. They came over and said, 'We want to pray for you.'"

At this point she didn't know that her husband was dying. Later, they sent her an audiotape that said, "We were trailing your car, and God told us to pull aside and pray for your husband." He had never made a verbal confession of Christ, at least not to his wife. "When you saw us, we had prayed for your husband, and we committed your husband to God."

The woman said to me, "I'm going to have confidence in that prayer." That was keeping her going. The situation was that her husband was dead. The faith was that God led someone to pull off the road just as the accident happened and pray, not for her, not for them, but for him. Isn't that amazing? What a God. That's who's alive in you and me. As we go out, those persons He has chosen for us to mingle with won't be able to resist that love.

God through us is interested only in what's best for the other person. Beloved, get that straight. Christ through you is not interested in what's best for you. That's hard. Christ through you, as He is using you, is interested only in what's best for the other person.

That's why there's a death in this life. There is a daily dying. We don't get up in the morning and try to die, but we daily recognize that we are dead. We're dead to those feelings and thoughts that pull us this way and that. And we're alive to the fact that Christ in us seeks what is best for someone else. That someone else is the person He has put in our lives today. It's not the indefinite somebody else that we don't know. He has a definite someone today in your life and my life.

I'm talking here about a quality of life and love that is characterized by rest. It is lived from the spirit, not the soul. If we haven't learned this yet, He's going to keep running experiences by us until we do. The only reason that's true is because you signed on. You told God you wanted to be His instrument, His vessel. The book of Hebrews says a real father chastens his kids. He corrects his kids. He wants what is best for his kids. He wants his kids to grow up and be adults, to take their proper place, to be an extension of the father.

God runs us through a maze of experiences that we still judge by our feelings and thoughts—our soul level. Then He runs us through some more. Finally, He brings us to the place where we have ceased from any activity that has its beginning point with us. We know we are experiencing Him in our inner being and, as with Elijah, He is quiet in us.

That's true knowing. And in that knowing we realize this: God is always after what's best for the other person. Judge everything in your life by that one rule, and you're on safe ground. A lot of times that will go against your feelings. That will go against your thoughts. But that's the dying to your feelings and thoughts so that life can come out. His life emerges.

We are going to see the same operation of the Father's life through us that we see in Jesus's life. The Father operated through the Son. We will see the life of the Father and the Son operating through us by the Holy Spirit. "As He is, so also are we in this world" (1 John 4:17). This isn't what we ought to be; this is what we are. We are the manifestors of poured-out life. The point of origin is not with us. We are simply manifestors. This is the fellowship of His sufferings that Paul longed to participate in (Philippians 3:10).

Sometimes you'll be called upon to be expendable in a situation, just as Jesus was. If so, whereas you were able many times to rescue someone else, you won't be able to save yourself. That is part of His suffering: to be an expendable commodity in the kingdom of God, just as God's own Son was expendable.

In our generation, the fellowship of the Spirit is often presented not as us being expendable but as us being exalted. But Jesus took off His outer garment, asked for a towel and a bowl of water, and washed His disciples' feet. The Son of God did that. I have to remind myself, that's who is alive in me. Washing feet doesn't look very earth-shaking or life-changing. But Almighty God pursued you and wooed you and enlisted you, not only to love you, but also to love through you. That kind of truth we can't despise. God is a lover through you. He is the kind of lover who doesn't need rewards, doesn't need applause, doesn't need acclaim, but loves for the sake of loving.

This world is crying out, but it doesn't know what it cries for. It cries for an intercessor. It cries for someone who bears the sufferings of Jesus, who is willing to stand in that place, be that light in the darkness, take that rebuff, and be the lamb that is sacrificed. Others will come to the Father someday and say, "Thank you for sending Mary or Bill or Joe. I learned about You through them." That's the way it works. God has imparted His divine life into your humanity. We are co-sons.

I know that most people associate intercession specifically with prayer, and that's fine. But I'm using intercession as Isaiah used it, speaking of Jesus:

> He poured out Himself to death,
> And was numbered with the transgressors;
> Yet He Himself bore the sin of many,
> And interceded for the transgressors
> (Isaiah 53:12).

How did He make intercession? With His life. He laid down His life. The spiritual father can't escape giving his own life. Spiritual little children and young men want to escape, and in the escape they show the power and deliverance of God. Spiritual fathers show the life of God in their willingness to be expendable. The father, who knows Him who is from the beginning, has moved into being an expression of the basic character of God. God's character is *agapē*—willed action for others—which makes us expendable.

> "Truly, truly, I say to you, unless a grain of wheat falls into the
> earth and dies, it remains alone; but if it dies, it bears much
> fruit" (John 12:24).

Our goal is for the living water to produce fruit in others, not to save us. He who saves his soul-life will lose it; he who loses his soul-life will save it. We are life-losers. We are expendable. We are here to be givers.

God has met all of our needs. He has brought us along this pilgrimage to a deep understanding of who we are so that He might spend us for others.

There is a cost to being an intercessor. What Paul said about the apostles applies here:

> God has exhibited us apostles last of all, as men condemned to death; because we have become a spectacle to the world, both to angels and to men. We are fools for Christ's sake…we are weak…we are without honor. To this present hour we are both hungry and thirsty, and are poorly clothed, and are roughly treated, and are homeless…we have become as the scum of the world, the dregs of all things (1 Corinthians 4:9-13).

I tell people, "Be careful about enlisting in this army. You'd better read these verses a few times before you sign up." Of course, if all we had to look forward to were these verses, that wouldn't be much to count on. But there is joy when God gives you an intercession. We used to say, "I'm going to get a blessing." But now we say, "I get a blessing when I see you blessed."

That's the joy. We endure the death so that the life can come to others. Then we receive the joy.

I've used a made-up illustration for several years. We know that Moses wasn't permitted to enter the Promised Land, even though he was the deliverer of the Jews. He took the children of Israel right to the banks of the Jordan River, but he couldn't go over. Being a preacher, I spiritualize that somewhat and say it's as though those Jewish children walked across the Jordan River on Moses's body, because he laid it down for them. Every time a little Jewish foot set land on the west side of the Jordan, you could hear Moses say, "Hallelujah! I couldn't go, but I was the way that all of them got to go."

Can't you hear Jesus? He's shouting in heaven over one that's saved. There have been millions, and He laid down His life for each one. You and I are the same. Our joy isn't that we get to set our foot down. Our joy is when we hear that other person say, "I know who I am." Or, "I know Christ." Or, "I've got victory." Then what we have taken by faith, we see manifested. And we praise our Father for His works of glory in the lives of others.

That's what we're all about, because we know Him on the father level. We know Him who is from the beginning. We know His purpose and His plan that through the Son, He is to have many sons and daughters who are to be the loving caretakers of His world, who are free to be expendable, to be poured out for others.

Before leaving this topic, it behooves us to circle back around to where this kind of love originates. John told us that "we love, because He first loved us" (1 John 4:19). Madame Guyon, the seventeenth-century French mystic, said if you really want to love the world, fasten your attention on how much you are loved. Fasten your attention on how much God loves you.

24

Loving God

A number of years ago, my daughter was going through a time of spiritual discouragement. We talked it out and I waited to see what the Lord was going to give me for her. The Lord then crystallized for me one of the purposes for which He may use these seasons in our lives. It has to do with loving God.

To set the mood for what I'm talking about here, let me tell you how I spent my days when I was home rather than on the road speaking. I know you could take this as an ought-to, but it's not. Chances are you've already tried something like it as an ought-to, and as an ought-to it doesn't work.

Barbara and I were then living in South Carolina. It was hot. So when I got up in the morning, I did the potentially sweat-producing things first before the heat of the day (because I am under the conviction there isn't any glory in perspiration). We had been working on the backyard, and with the help of others had succeeded in turning a jungle into a small, respectable back lawn.

Every day I would first get the broom and sweep whatever needed to be swept. Things are always falling out of trees down there. It's amazing the amount of junk that can descend on a little concrete in 24 hours, but it did every day. Then I'd rake the gravel path that went through the lawn. I would get down and pick all the weeds out of that gravel. After the backyard was tidy, I would sit down and drink a glass of grapefruit juice and read the paper. Then I went for a walk, three to five miles depending on the route.

Barbara had a job that started at 10:00, so while she was finishing getting ready for work, I would work the daily crossword puzzle. I had this chair—my favorite chair—which I was in by 9:30 to do the puzzle. There wasn't any sense in trying to do any spiritual reading before I completed the crossword puzzle. I fought that battle long enough, as if it were more spiritual to do the spiritual stuff first and then do the crossword puzzle. The thing that was on my mind was the crossword puzzle, so I did it first.

About the time Barbara was ready to go to work, I was through. I had everything done. I could spend the rest of the day as I pleased. So there I'd be, in my chair. I would lean my chair back and I was in heaven. I had my pens and paper next to me, different copies of Scripture, and spiritual books that I'd be delving into. On one side of me was one small bookcase, and behind me was another, and I had all my favorite books there. I was in my world.

Sometimes I'd just reach back and see what book I might pick out. What does the Lord want to read today? Madame Guyon, Teresa of Avila, Oswald Chambers. Deeper life books.

I had already decided that He wanted me to read certain ones, but sometimes He would have a surprise for me. What did I want to do first that day? I wanted to read the Scriptures. Or I wanted to read Oswald Chambers. About the only interruption I had was Barbara coming home for lunch, so about 12:15 I would get lunch ready. After she left, I would go out and see if any more magnolia leaves had dropped in the backyard. Then I'd go back inside to my chair, and I'd have from 1:00 until 5:00 in the chair. I did a lot more reading. A lot more thinking. And I trusted that the Lord spoke to me.

This little illustration is about just loving God—fellowshipping with God by oneself. It ties back into what the Lord showed me regarding my daughter. She was expressing pain about her temporary condition in her walk with the Lord. In particular, she was struggling that God never seems to hear. God never seems to care. God never seems to answer. Have you ever been there? A word for her didn't come immediately, but the next day I said, "Dear, do you suppose that we are to love God the same way He loves us?" Paul wrote to the Romans:

> For while we were still helpless, at the right time Christ died for the ungodly. For one will hardly die for a righteous man; though perhaps for the good man someone would dare even to die. But God demonstrates His own love toward us, in that while we were yet sinners, Christ died for us (5:6-8).

We were loved before any of us ever made any overture to God. God loved us and He didn't get anything back at that point. He wasn't getting anything back from humanity when we fell. He was loving without any reward. He only loved.

There isn't any reward system in God's love. He loves because He is love, not because of what He gets in return. But there has been and still is a whole lot of reward system in the kind of love we're often taught in the Christian faith. What else can we expect? There is a reward system in fleshly love. We love because we are going to get something for loving.

In our spiritual pilgrimage, we want God to stroke us. Bless us. Give us something. Reward us. As little children in the faith, we very much wanted a reward system. Even further along in our Christian pilgrimage, we have still wanted that. When you and I are in some temporary pit, we want that. The flesh wants a reward system.

But God just loves. He would love if in all of recorded history no one had ever turned to love Him back. His nature is to love. He can't do anything else.

As I hammered through this that weekend with my daughter, I finally said to her, "Do you know what Roman 5:5 says? It says the love of God has been poured out within our hearts. And 1 John 2:12-14 says that we now know the Father. Do you think that some of this pain you and others go through, where you don't seem to get any strokes from God, is part of the process whereby the real love that He has poured out in your heart comes out? So that you'll be able to love Him with that love? His own love loving Him back."

You and I want to love God if He'll bless us. We want to love Him if He'll save our children. We want to love Him if He'll provide us with a lovely home or if we can keep all of our things. We want to love Him, but we think He ought to be doing something for us in return.

But there is a deeper level, an inner knowing for you and me, where we just fall in love with God because He is God. We love God in the same way God loves us. He didn't have to learn to do it; He can't help but do it. So also we can't help but love Him.

A Scripture illustrates what I'm talking about. Jesus said to Thomas, "Blessed are those who have not seen, and yet have believed" (John 20:29 NKJV). That's what I'm alluding to. All the strokes God gives us are, in a way, seeing and feeling. They are God proving to us that He's on the job: jerking our chestnuts out of the fire, lifting the depression off, doing this, doing that.

But if God is working in our lives to take us deeper in an experience of loving Him, then some of our prior ways that may have proven very satisfactory in the past will have to go. How do you move on to a new thing as long as the old is still life to you? As long as the old is still ministering something to us, we don't readily move on. Who wants to leave what's good? Who wants to leave what's working?

So God calls a halt to one chapter in your life. You say, "What's this all about?" God replies, "It's in order to start another chapter in your life." Then He calls a halt to the new chapter in order to begin another one after that. If God has poured out His love into you, with which you are to love Him back, then His love through you back to Him will be the kind of love that won't have any demands upon it. God must be true to Himself. So as He lives in us, His expression of love back to Himself must be true to His character, which is just to love.

Here is a whole vista open to us. I really don't think most of us know a great deal about loving God. What if there is a way to deepen our love experience of God? What if we've exhausted all the energy-expending ways we've been shown, but haven't investigated a whole new way of exploring and knowing God?

Some people go into monasteries or convents to withdraw from the whole world and focus on God. With our Western civilization's busy, busy attitude toward life, that may appear to us as one of the greatest wastes of time we could imagine. I was chatting with someone about that and a thought crossed my mind. I said, "You know, the vocation of prayer and meditation and love for God *is* their work. What if that love, devotion, and prayer being done by many, many people that we don't even know scattered around the world—who may appear to be shirking responsibility—were actually staying the wrath of God on the planet Earth? That would be a noble work, would it not?"

I think it's hard for us to believe that maybe God's main objective would be that we just love Him. We think that God's main objective is that we save the world. To just love God seems like a waste of time to a busy person. And yet when we start reading those psalms that mean the most to us, most of them are nothing but the psalmist's expression of love and adoration to God. We talk about knowing God. What better way to know God than to fall in love with Him—without Him having to reward you?

To use the language of 1 John, this is the father stage of loving God. In the little children and young men stages, the emphasis is on ourselves and what we do. But in the father stage, the emphasis is on Him: "You know Him who has been from the beginning." Our focus shifts from ourselves to the Father. What we will discover is that to experience the love of God at this depth will be the most spirit- and soul-satisfying experience possible. Jesus said, "This is eternal life, that they may know You, the only true God, and Jesus Christ whom You have sent" (John 17:3).

To really know God is not just to know all these things about God. To truly know and love someone defies description. I didn't tell my wife why I loved her. I just said, "I love you." I didn't love her because. I just loved her.

Love is its own end. To love and be loved, that is the essence of the kingdom.

To love and be loved.

25

Entering God's Rest

We live in one of the two most high-paced societies on earth (some claim Japan is even worse). Most of us rush to get out the door in the morning so that we can sit in rush-hour traffic, so that we can endure a hectic and stressful day at work, so that we can get back into rush-hour traffic, so that we can grab a meal on the way home, or, if we have children, fix dinner, help with homework, and get them off to bed, so that we can have 15 minutes of "quality" time to ourselves or with our spouse before we drop off to sleep, exhausted.

Visitors from Europe, accustomed to shorter workdays, a minimum of four weeks' vacation, and stores closed on Sundays, are typically astounded at the pace of American life. "When do you Americans stop and enjoy life?" they ask.

In addition to our frenetic lifestyle, most believers feel slightly guilty most of the time because we're never quite able to get our act together. We never have good enough quiet times or devotionals, do enough Bible study, pray enough, witness enough, or reduce our bad thoughts and feelings enough to really please God. Starting next week we'll try harder.

In contrast, the writer to the Hebrews said,

So there remains a Sabbath rest for the people of God (4:9).

Just reading those words makes your soul slow and quiet down, doesn't it? There remains a rest for the people of God. God has provided a rest for us. It's not in the sweet by-and-by. It's for now.

The author of Hebrews uses the Jews' approaching Canaan to illustrate God's rest. God offered the Jews rest in the Promised Land. But the first time around, they didn't enter in. Later, Joshua did lead the people into the Promised Land, and they experienced a taste of God's rest. But it was just a shadow of the real thing, an illustration for us, because the real thing could be fulfilled only in Christ.

> Therefore, let us fear if, while a promise remains of entering His rest, any one of you may seem to have come short of it… For if Joshua had given them rest, He would not have spoken of another day after that. So there remains a Sabbath rest for the people of God (4:1,8-9).

That last statement makes it obvious that the folks the book of Hebrews was written to had not found God's rest. If it remains to be found, you haven't found it. Most of us are still rest-seekers. The lack of rest within us proves that we really haven't entered *His* rest.

I was a rest-seeker for years. For a long, long time I thought the rest was just a kind of passive existence. I wanted to go to a retreat and get somebody to take care of me so I could get out of my regular routine and shift into neutral. I called that rest. But that wasn't rest.

My concept of rest was external because my inner knowing wasn't any deeper than that. My inner knowing was still just me. I didn't have any spiritual awareness deeper than an awareness of myself. And since that was my deepest awareness, I had to make myself look acceptable before I could possibly be at rest. So I tried to stop my soul fluctuations, which God never meant us to stop. It was all based on my works, my efforts. I couldn't be at rest that way, because I was trying to do something that was foreign to God's plan for my life. If we're constantly trying to stop an activity within us that God has put into motion, then we never will know rest.

But we are meant to know God's rest. The writer to the Hebrews said, "Therefore let us be diligent to enter that rest" (4:11). We are supposed to enter in. And he tells us the key to entering God's rest: "For the one who has entered [God's] rest has himself also rested from his works, as God did from His" (4:10).

The key to entering God's rest is not to cease from all activity. Rather, the key is to cease from labor that has its beginning point with us. We rest from *our* works. We rest from activity that has its origin with *us*. If we haven't ceased from that, we haven't entered into God's rest. Jesus instructed us,

> "Come to Me, all who are weary and heavy-laden, and I will give you rest. Take My yoke upon you and learn from Me, for I am gentle and humble in heart, and you will find rest for your souls. For My yoke is easy and My burden is light" (Matthew 11:28-30).

We have lived the Christian life as a struggle. It's not meant to be a struggle. It's meant to be a rest. We enter that rest when we learn to live as Jesus lived: from the life of Another within us and out through us. Until then, we try to reproduce a life that's foreign to us. But in the intimate union of our spirit with God's Spirit, that life will be spontaneously reproduced. The life that comes forth from us is the life of God. That yoke is easy, not difficult. That burden is light, not heavy. We find rest for our soul.

I'm not saying that you won't have any fluctuations in your soul, in your thoughts and your feelings, but I am saying that deep within you you'll be at rest. You'll have inner peace because you'll be walking out the life God has invited you to participate in with Him.

What does it take to rest from our own works, as God did from His? The same thing it took for the Jews to enter the Promised Land: faith.

> So we see that they were not able to enter because of unbelief.
>
> Therefore, let us fear if, while a promise remains of entering His rest, any one of you may seem to have come short of it. For indeed we have had good news preached to us, just as they also; but the word they heard did not profit them, because it was not united by faith in those who heard. For we who have believed enter that rest (Hebrews 3:19–4:3).

By faith we rest in what God has already done in the unseen and eternal realm within us. He has made us His holy, blameless, irreproachable children. He has made us the righteousness of God in Christ. Our old man died with Christ. We have been raised with Christ as completely new creations, born of God's Spirit. He has made us perfect in His sight. There is no condemnation. He has become one with our spirit, through which He manifests His life to the world. He is pleased with us. He delights in us. He loves us. He lives His life as us.

The seen and temporal realm doesn't tell us these things. God reveals them to us by His Word and His Spirit, to our spirit. That's why we find that famous verse, Hebrews 4:12, at the end of this exhortation to enter God's rest:

> For the word of God is living and active and sharper than any two-edged sword, and piercing as far as the division of soul and spirit, of both joints and marrow, and able to judge the thoughts and intentions of the heart.

Usually that verse is quoted in isolation. But it was written in the context of entering God's rest. The point is this: we can't enter God's rest as long as we are living on soul-based appearances and feelings instead of God's spirit realities. We rest on what God has already done in the unseen and eternal.

So how can we be diligent to enter God's rest?

Quit trying.

Say, "Lord, I desire to be in Your rest. Your Word says I am in your rest. I believe Your Word. I am in You and You are in me." Now, let that be. You can do that, can't you? There's no sweating and striving and straining in that.

We're no longer driven by the compulsions of what we ought to be or do. If we are, we're not using God's yardstick. God declares us holy and blameless and beautiful in His sight. We are not to strive. We are to be. That's the good news. We already are. *You* already are.

Turn your eye—your spiritual eye—inward. But don't stop the inward look at the soul, at the feelings and the thoughts that have controlled and dominated your life for as many years as you can probably remember. Rather, rest in that spiritual center God placed in humanity, where God could meet His creature.

Since you came to Jesus Christ, your human spirit has always wanted to flower and bring forth life. God may have waited for this moment to enlighten that receiver spirit of yours and begin to calm your soul with His rest. He says, "I bought you with a price. I am one with you. I implanted my Spirit within your spirit, and I will live My life through you."

When you enter into that, you breathe a sigh of relief. You say, "I'm home. I'm home. I'm back with the One who made me for Himself. I'm back to my real, original, true purpose for having been created in the beginning. I'm back with my true spiritual Father, before humanity was kidnapped and blinded. The kidnapper said that ultimate reality is the seen and temporal. If I can't see it, taste it, touch it, smell it, or handle it, it isn't real. But My Father tells me that if I can see it, taste it, touch it, smell it, or handle it, it isn't ultimate, spirit reality. It's created. It has a life expectancy and then it's over. What's ultimately real is the unseen and eternal."

> We look not at the things which are seen, but at the things which are not seen; for the things which are seen are temporal, but the things which are not seen are eternal (2 Corinthians 4:18).

Oswald Chambers wrote, "You mind the journey inward, and God will see that rivers of living water will flow out of you." I had that reversed for so long. Didn't you? I thought I had to make sure the rivers of living water were flowing out, then I would know I had an acceptable relationship with God. But that's not it. Mind the kingdom within, and out of you will flow rivers of living water.

To people already born again, Paul wrote, "My children, with whom I am again in labor until Christ is formed in you" (Galatians 4:19). Jesus already lived in them. They already had the Spirit. Yet Paul wanted them to fully experience Christ being formed inside them.

The trip we are on isn't outward. It's inward. Jesus said the kingdom of God is within you (Luke 17:21). Paul said your body is a temple of the

Holy Spirit (1 Corinthians 6:19). Jesus promised that He and the Father would come and take up their abode in you (John 14:23). Your spirit is the place of the divine habitation while you're here on earth. Your spirit is the place to be cultivating. Go within! Go within! Go within! The more God takes you within, the more people will see Him in you.

We are all that we were ever meant to be: one with the One who is life. We learn to live in the Holy of Holies within us. In that place of His habitation we encounter only one Person beside ourselves, and we fellowship with Him there. When we experience our true union, we enter into a knowing of the All in all, Who is life, Whom to know is life everlasting.

Scientists tell us the universe is at least 90 billion trillion miles across, and expanding. I believe that as expansive as the physical universe is, and as much as is yet to be discovered externally, equally so is the expanse of God within. We are on a lifelong—no, eternal—pilgrimage of discovering and knowing God and His nature, His love, His ways.

Along the way of that pilgrimage, we drop the outer things one by one. They lie strewn along the road behind us, no longer useful for the journey. They were all prefaced by the pronoun *my*. My wife, my husband, my children, my home, my job, my friends, my church. They gave us our identity. But we have shifted to a new source of identity. In the end, God can give us back many of the things we had to lose along the way, because we don't need them anymore. They are no longer life to us. Christ is our life, and we will settle for nothing less.

Now we are truly liberated. We are God's free persons. We can have the world's possessions and it's okay. We can lack the world's possessions and it's okay. We can have status and it's okay. We can lack status and it's okay. We can be with people or with no one and it's okay. With Paul, we "have learned to be content in whatever circumstances" we are in (Philippians 4:11). We reign with Him in life.

One time I led a retreat in Michigan for the staff members of a conference center. On the last morning, we had communion. The conference center leader served us the bread and the wine and talked about Jesus saying, "Eat My body and drink My blood." As I partook of the bread and the wine, the Spirit seemed to say to me, "You see, Dan, all I have to give you is Me. It's represented right here. All I have to give you is Me."

That's the good news. It's not religion. It's not us doing something to earn God's approval. It's His giving us Himself. It's "Christ in you, the hope of glory." That's rest. To be in Him is to be in perfect oneness. To be in Him is to be at rest.

It's an inner life and nothing else. *Nothing else.* If we pursue the externals, they become idols to us. We'll worship them. And we'll miss the life.

There is a place of quiet rest, but it isn't in this world. There is a place of quiet rest, but it isn't in your senses. There is a place of quiet rest, but it isn't in your soul. There is a place of quiet rest. It's in God.

In the month before she died, Barbara was sleeping a lot because of her medication. One day she woke up out of a groggy sleep and lay there with something obviously on her mind. Finally she turned to me and said, "Dan, whenever you speak now, just talk about the unseen."

"Why?" I asked.

"That's all that's real."

She ought to have known by then. She was close to crossing over. Beloved, that's all that's real. That is all that's real.

About the Authors

Dan Stone was a graduate of Southern Baptist Theological Seminary and served as a pastor for 16 years and in administration at Georgetown College and Samford University. He traveled the US sharing the message of "Christ in you" for more than 20 years. He authored the Union Life Ministries book *The Mystery of the Gospel*, as well as numerous articles and booklets. He finished his earthly course in 2005 and joined his Lord in heaven.

David Gregory is the author of several books, including the *New York Times'* bestseller *Dinner with a Perfect Stranger* and Christy Award finalist *The Last Christian*. David earned master's degrees from Dallas Theological Seminary and the University of North Texas. He now writes full-time and lives in the Pacific Northwest.

Grace Walk
What You've Always Wanted in the Christian Life
Steve McVey

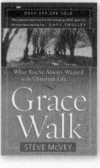

Now with a fresh cover! The nearly 200,000-selling *Grace Walk* has helped thousands of believers leave behind the "manic-depressive" Christian walk: either running around trying to perform to be acceptable to God or thinking they've failed Him again and wondering if they'll ever measure up.

Living the *grace walk* gets Christians off this religious roller coaster. Using his own journey from legalism into grace, Steve McVey illustrates the foundational, biblical truths of who believers are in Jesus Christ and how they can let Him live His life through them each day.

As they experience their identity in Jesus Christ, Christians will come to know "Amazing Grace" as not just a song but as their true way of life.

Classic Christianity
Life's Too Short to Miss the Real Thing
Bob George

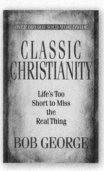

The breakthrough book that has helped over half a million Christians worldwide since 1989!

Classic Christianity—Bob George's eye-opening distillation of the life-transforming truths of the gospel—now has a fresh cover and interior that reflect the up-to-the-minute relevance of its message.

Like so many Christians, Bob George started out in love with Jesus, only to end up feeling disappointed and empty. Drawing on his struggles and his teaching and counseling experience, Bob cuts to the heart of believers' common questions...

- Doesn't God expect me to clean up my act before I approach Him?
- I know God loves me—but does He *accept* me?
- I'm saved and forgiven...do I just wait for heaven now?

In *Classic Christianity*, believers will see the way back to the life Jesus provided—a life set free from the law's bondage, lived in the newness of the Spirit, and secure in the Father's affection.

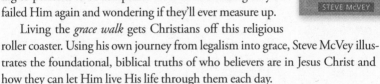